FORTUNE FAVORS THE BRAVE

FORTUNE FAVORS THE BRAVE

FUJITSU: THIRTY YEARS IN COMPUTERS

Taiyu Kobayashi

Chairman of the Board
FUJITSU LIMITED

Translated by Richard Cleary

TOYO KEIZAI SHINPOSHA

Tokyo

Printed in Japan by TOYO KEIZAI Printing Co.

PREFACE

The whys and wherefores I cannot explain but the history of Fujitsu is my history. These thirty years I have been involved with computers: at first in computer development, later in sales and operations, and finally as an executive of the company. Today, Fujitsu stands at the top of Japan's computer industry. The path that led to our present success was certainly not an easy one. There were rugged slopes to climb, sheer cliffs to scale, and mazes to find our way through. Nevertheless, the combined efforts of many Fujitsu employees brought us to the top.

The domestic and international economic climate and increasingly competitive market place have made it difficult, but thanks to the recent surge in office automation, demand for our computers, word processors and other products have increased sharply and Fujitsu has continued to achieve steady growth. The new age before us, however, will require men younger than myself to lead. Having decided it was time to turn over the leadership in June of 1981, I passed the baton to Takuma Yamamoto. He took over the responsibilities of President and I assumed the title of Chairman.

I was looking forward to having a little free time and being able to indulge myself with the gardening I so enjoy when a publishing company, the Toyo Keizai Shinposha, approached me with the suggestion I write a book. They encouraged me to write a "living company history" of Fujitsu. I have been asked over the years to give a great number of speeches; writing books, however, is not one of my strong points. Nevertheless, thanks to the cooperation of many people I have been able to publish this book. Especially, the cooperation of Mr. K. Akagi of Toyo Keizai Shinposha and the devotion of Mr. R. Cleary have been indispensable.

Computers today are no longer only a tool for science and business: They are finding their way into people's homes. Nothing would please me more than if many different people, not just Fujitsu people, read this and learn something of the history of computers in Japan.

Taiyu Kobayashi

CONTENTS

FORTUNE FAVORS THE BRAVE

FUJITSU: THIRTY YEARS IN COMPUTERS

I

FIRST TRIUMPH

Negotiations in Australia are returned to the starting line due to the "computer-gate" incident. Three years later, with a re-submitted bid, Fujitsu gains a marvelous victory—our first triumph in international competition.

THE ASAHI'S BIG SCOOP

"Fujitsu's Large Scale Mainframes Defeat IBM. Contract Signed With Australia."

Waking early as usual on October 25, 1977, I went to the front door, as was my custom, to get the morning paper. Returning to the living room, I sat down and opened the morning edition of the *Asahi*. The next instant I was on my feet. There, in bold headlines on the front page, was just what I had feared. A journalist from the *Asahi*'s economics desk had released some potentially explosive news. The article in the *Asahi Shimbun*, a daily with one of the largest circulations in Japan, threatened to upset the bid evaluation process then taking place in Australia.

"Now he has done it, writing it up like this after I specifically asked him not to," I muttered to myself. At the time, Fujitsu, through our subsidiary, Fujitsu Australia, had tendered a bid to the Australian Commonwealth government for a major computer network installation. It was a large project involving the government's Bureau of Statistics

3

(ABS) and the Trade and Resources Department (DTR). They planned joint use of a new mainframe computer installation for processing trade and financial statistics, census analysis and related work, as well as the complete renovation of the existing national network. Total cost for the project was expected to be six billion yen.

The February 1977 bidding included Control Data (whose equipment they were then using), as well as proposals from International Business Machines (IBM) and Univac. Fujitsu had also submitted a bid. By May, three months later, the field had been narrowed down to two companies, IBM and Fujitsu. The *Asahi's News'* "scoop" had come at a very critical point in the Australian deliberations.

The latter half of the 1970's saw Japan's core industries represented by steel, autos, and television sets gain decisive competitive strength internationally. As these Japanese products flowed into the U.S. and European markets, trade friction became a serious problem. When it came to high technology industries such as computers, however, questions remained as to whether Japan had finally caught up to the U.S. on this level. It was still not at all unusual for Japan to lose in international competition in this arena. The situation with respect to the bidding for the Australian project was different: we were now confident that we were going to "beat IBM."

Information had recently come to me that the informal decision in the evaluation process appeared to be in favor of Fujitsu. Nevertheless, should word of this be leaked before the formal announcement, I feared it might upset the process and thus tried to keep it quiet. The fact was, the *Asahi* journalist had come to me to gather information a few days earlier. He had heard that "... The Australian decision had been made in favor of Fujitsu." He said his source was reliable and that he planned to publish his story. Startled, but feigning ignorance, I replied, "I am afraid I can't confirm the story."

Putting on a smile, he repeatedly insisted that the information he possessed was accurate. I suppressed the urge to ask him various questions regarding the route by which the information had come to him. If I asked too many questions I ran the risk of getting caught up in the excitement of his account. "That's news I'm very glad to hear," I said calmly, "and just suppose for a moment that unofficially it has been decided in favor of Fujitsu. Should it be published, it could do great harm. In negotiations like these, until the signed contract is firmly in hand, a careless leak can scuttle the whole business any time right up to the final moment. It happens all too often! Please refrain from writing any of this."

"Don't worry," he assured me, "There is absolutely no room for doubt. I'm told that in Australia it has been 'definitely determined' so there is no possibility of repercussions."

Listening to him, I thought to myself, "Well, it looks like it's finally over." Although this news was not something I had leaked, but information he had obtained from a first-hand source, it still might not prove to be conclusive. Yet, in spite of our conversation and my cautioning, the journalist wrote it up as though everything had been decided.

I put the newspaper aside, finished the breakfast my wife prepared for me, and left for the office at the usual time. There was no point now in getting all excited, raising a ruckus, or making a scene. When I arrived at the office I called those involved to a meeting and announced that the deal, despite what had been published, might well fall through. I later learned that the information the *Asahi* journalist put in print had previously passed into the hands of other companies.

There is another element I should mention: There was a special reason for choosing that particular day, October 25th, to publish the story. IBM executives from all over the world were gathered in Japan and had planned a meeting for that day. On the evening of the 25th, the Japan Electronic Industry Development Association (JEIDA) was holding a party and Frank T. Cary, then IBM Chairman, was expected to attend. The article was timed for this occasion.

It may be that the journalist wanted to see the troubled expression on the IBM chairman's face after having been defeated by Japan in international competition. In fact, I was the one who ended up being the most troubled.

As I was about to enter the reception hall at the Hotel Okura that evening, I spotted the journalist. He looked a bit sheepish but it was hardly the proper place for me to lose my temper, so without saying a word I proceeded into the hall. The reporters could not enter the reception area; they seemed to be congregating in the corridor waiting eagerly to see what would happen. I tried to be as inconspicuous as possible and stood quietly off toward a corner of the room.

"Chairman Cary has been asking where the Fujitsu President, Kobayashi is. He is looking for you," a business friend informed me when he noticed me in the corner. I could not very well say, "Sorry, I'd rather not," so I was obliged to approach Mr. Cary and shake hands. He does not have a large build for an American, but he projects a feeling of "dominance." He never raised the subject of the Australian bids. Yet, he must have been vexed.

Although it cannot be stated conclusively that the *Asahi* "scoop" and IBM's counter-offensive were the only causes, just as I feared, the decision making process, which had reached the stage of an informal determination in favor of Fujitsu, was abandoned, and the whole thing returned to square one. This reversal, involving what became known as the "computer-gate incident," produced in me a tremendous feeling of regret. It was the disappointment of "letting the big one get away." There was also a feeling of resentment toward the journalist who shall remain unnamed.

"COMPUTER-GATE"

On January 4th, 1978, the year following the October "news-scoop," the office was enveloped in a festive atmosphere. Fujitsu women came to work with their hair done-up in traditional styles and dressed in bright kimonos. It is the custom in Japan for women employees to wear traditional kimono on the first day of work of the new year. They look especially beautiful at this time.

I was taking care of some routine matters in my office when an international call came in from Australia. This was the onset of the political controversy over the Australian government's Bureau of Statistics' (ABS) computer system bidding process—better known as the "computer-gate incident." It was the incident which upset Fujitsu's successful bid—a bid which had been informally accepted—and forced the whole process back to the starting gate.

Throughout the world, governments are an extremely important market for the EDP (Electronic Data Processing) industry. Australia is no exception. With its great size, it is a country rich in natural resources. The population and industry are concentrated around the capital, Canberra, in the south-east. The private sector EDP market, however, is not that large, and there is no Australian computer manufacturer. The government or public sector market in Australia, considering the size of the information systems required, is an extremely attractive one for computer suppliers. Public sector markets in general are so important that the percentage of a government market held has become something of a status symbol among computer manufacturers.

With this in mind, when the Australian government announced they were planning the purchase of a computer system (EDP system) on a scale not likely to be seen again anywhere over the next decade, it was no surprise that competing companies went into high gear in a frantic race to obtain the contract. IBM, in particular, claiming that they had "nurtured and developed the Australian computer market," felt that they had to capture the order.

Four companies, including Fujitsu, tendered bids. I have already mentioned that the field was finally narrowed down to two designated bidders: Fujitsu and IBM. After the *Asahi Shimbun* article appeared, we received no communication of any kind from Australia. Months passed, and soon it was the mid-summer Christmas and holiday season down under. A rumor began to circulate regarding the reason for the delay in designating the successful bidder. The winner, by this time, should have already been determined. It was said that the final decision was being delayed because Prime Minister Frazer had raised an objection to adopting Fujitsu's FACOM system. The reason for the objection appeared to be that FACOM Australia had employed an official who had once been a member of the government's ABS Systems Select Committee, and IBM Australia, our competitor, had sent a letter calling this into question.

This rumor was clearly a thrust directed at Fujitsu. It was of such a nature that we could not simply remain silent. Yet, it was only a rumor: there was no party against whom we could register an official protest, nothing concrete to go on. At FACOM Australia there were anxious brainstorming meetings, but little prospect of a good plan of action emerging from these sessions.

The international call from Australia on January 4th was a request that I, as president of the parent company, "send a telegram of official protest to Prime Minister Frazer." Whether it was appropriate for me, from a different country and not directly involved, to wire a protest to the Prime Minister was not a question that could be quickly resolved. I responded to their request that I would examine alternatives and get back to them.

Naturally, our internal analysis of the situation yielded a divergence of opinions regarding the proposed direct response. First of all, the information was based on rumor, not something publicly acknowledged. Was it at all proper to send a protest on grounds such as these? Second, if an executive of a company in the private sector of a foreign country were to issue a protest regarding a situation that the Prime Minister himself was thought to be involved in, would this be considered interfering in the politics of another country? Third, assuming we did protest, would the politicians and bureaucrats in the Prime Minister's circle give the matter fair treatment?

All things considered, I instructed our Australian subsidiary to make the following points in a "protest" to the Australian government:

1. If, in fact, the cause of the delay in the final decision was a suspicion involving Fujitsu, we would ask that everything be made public and request an impartial evaluation.

2. So much time and money had already been spent during the evaluation process that for it to go down the drain due to some dubious "suspicion" would profit neither

the honorable Australian government nor the public at large. The "suspicions" must be cleared up as quickly as possible.

3. The problematic "employment of an ex-government official" was accomplished with the cooperation and understanding of all the related government agencies. This can be clearly proven. Therefore, we think the true value of the system submitted for evaluation should be appraised, and the decision reached as quickly as possible.

OUR FIRST TRIUMPH OVER IBM

In the competitive bidding for the Bureau of Statistics contract only those computers which already had a proven track record of operation in Australia could be included in the tendered bid. Our largest computer at the time, the FACOM M-190, was already being used by the Commonwealth Scientific and Industrial Research Organization (CSIRO), a government research institute where it was very highly regarded. The cost-performance rating in particular was judged to be excellent. On this point, in any event, we were not to be defeated by IBM.

To buttress this record of achievement, we employed an ex-government official in order to better understand local conditions and requirements. There was no way we could anticipate that this would develop into the problem described above. Our objective was to tap this individual's knowledge; there was, of course, absolutely no involvement in the government's bid selection process. Allegations made by IBM were false. It should also be noted that Prime Minister Frazer was facing an election and was loath to be saddled with even the slightest hint of impropriety. This is probably why he ordered the bids be re-submitted.

In any event, my instructions for the protest carried a rather strong tone. I was confident that Fujitsu's FACOM M-190 was superior to the IBM 370-180III which our opponent was thought to be proposing. This confidence was strengthened by the fact that our performance, including reliability, computation speed, etc., with respect to cost, as well as degree of satisfaction with our support and maintenance service, had already convinced people in government of our superiority.

Nevertheless, should the whole thing become politicized, it would become a totally different ball game. Since there was every possibility this is just what would happen, I cautioned the executives of our Australian subsidiary: "If it evolves into a political controversy, make absolutely sure you do not get drawn into it."

Our fears were borne out less than two weeks after the January 4th phone call. The respected Melbourne newspaper, *The Age*, published an exclusive article, "The Rumor is True," and all at once the competition became a political issue. I was told it was the top story on network television news throughout Australia.

At this point, with charge and counter charge being bandied about, Frazer could not very well have the contract awarded to Fujitsu. Finally, in cabinet, he ordered that the present recommendations be scrapped and announced that new tenders had to be called. This was on February 9th, 1978. At the opening session of Parliament the next day, an opposition party member even suggested, "Could it be that Prime Minister Frazer received a payoff from IBM and moved to squelch Fujitsu's bid?" Parliament apparently spent two weeks just spinning its wheels and got nowhere with the problem.

The press immediately dubbed the affair "computer-gate," in a play on President Nixon's "Watergate." This was due to the suspicion that the Prime Minister's decision might have been influenced by some form of activity on the part of IBM. From a purely political perspective, with the majority and minority parties about evenly matched and an election approaching, it was essential for Frazer to avoid even the appearance of impropriety within his administration.

The mass media played up the incident. The uproar, which by and large ignored Fujitsu—one of the principle parties—and failed to provoke debate on the merits of the computer systems involved, turned out to be a "computergate" minus the computers. In the end, although Fujitsu had obtained the recommendation of the original evaluation committee, new tenders were called for without the reason for overturning the initial decision ever being made clear. Once the new tenders were called for, and we had again submitted our bid, the Australians, profiting from their bitter previous experience, enforced strict gag orders. We could obtain absolutely no information. This was the case not only for Fujitsu; it must have been the same for IBM.

I was nervous and impatient. Even after the point where it felt like the decision would be announced any day, there was no word. Queries to those directly in charge at Fujitsu Australia always brought the same reply, "We just don't know." In spite of this communications blackout, I was firmly convinced that the best product would inevitably win.

It was generally believed that IBM had submitted a new, high performance model, the IBM 3033, in their second tender. However, it had no track record in Australia. Since the Australian government weighed previous performance history heavily in its evaluation, the fact that it was a new model probably would not work in its favor. At least, that was my optimistic appraisal.

Then, in November, 1979, without any preliminary indications, we received notification: "It has been decided in favor of Fujitsu." The happiness of that moment cannot be described. The decision had been delayed two years, but twice in succession the laurels had gone to Fujitsu. "Fujitsu fought IBM well and garnered the final victory. They have tremendous capability." Accolades were heard from Australia and around the world. Because it fortunately all ended so well, the particulars can now be related lightheartedly. It had been a tense, anxious period in my life.

I should mention that Fujitsu Australia was the last of the eight computer companies to get started there, and consequently had the smallest market share. At the time, there were approximately 2000 general purpose computers in operation in the Australian market. IBM held a 60% share of the market. The British company ICL (International Computers Ltd.), with the help of old commonwealth ties, was putting up a spirited fight. Our computers were thus constrained to struggle against heavy odds.

Our strategy for somehow penetrating and gaining market share was based on a thoroughgoing localization: The Fujitsu Australia president was an Australian and there were only seven Japanese employees (4%). Close collaboration with the parent company presented substantial difficulties. Everyone worked very hard to resolve them. Words cannot begin to describe the kind of effort I know they exerted. This victory afforded them great joy.

I certainly do not think, by the way, that this was by any means the "final victory." Rather, I like to believe that to observers throughout the world this was clearly just the beginning of victory. Perhaps we should say it was the first

successful international step on the course charted by
Fujitsu President, Kanjiro Okada, who in 1966 began the
campaign for "high reliability."

In the afterglow of this triumph, in 1980, we received an
order for a comprehensive on-line system and host mainframe computer from the Australian central bank,
The Reserve Bank of Australia. We now had consecutive
victories over IBM!

LESSONS

The Fujitsu Australia President, M. P. Rydon once
jokingly remarked that "Thanks to this ['computer-gate']
incident our FACOM trade name has reached every part of
the country." There are, however, three points regarding
this incident that I have deep feelings about. First of all,
I was greatly impressed by the high level of the Australian
people's public consciousness. Despite all the commotion, it
never degenerated into an emotional argument, nor was
there ever any unfair public debate with overtones of racial
prejudice. Public opinion focused on treating IBM and
Fujitsu fairly, and I am grateful for the sympathetic understanding we received from beginning to end.

Second, as a result of the incident, everything, beginning
with the bid specifications which were rewritten, had to be
done over. This meant a tremendous reinvestment of time,
money and energy right up to when the new bids were
accepted in November, 1979. However, the objective I
emphasized in my directives to Fujitsu Australia, that any
suspicion be completely resolved openly in the public eye,
was, the form it took notwithstanding, generally realized. In
a political controversy it is all too easy to become involved in
behind-the-scenes dealing. Nevertheless, other than Fujitsu

Australia's repeated appeals based on my instructions, we intently maintained our silence and were not drawn into the fray. We avoided making the content of our protest public and thus kept our distance from the political controversy. It is very likely that we managed to keep public opinion on our side because we emphasized "no impropriety" at every opportunity.

Third, our appeal to question the real value and judge accordingly bore magnificent fruit during the second bidding process. A third party evaluation committee was commissioned and a thoroughly impartial evaluation conducted. Since, during the interim, IBM had announced the 3033, a high performance system, it is safe to assume it was this model that was submitted. Nonetheless, it was Fujitsu that won.

Although Australia has no national computer manufacturer, in terms of computer utilization it must be included among the leading nations of the world. Its computer market is expanding at an annual rate of about twenty percent. The tempo is such that the intensity and severity of competition is the same as in other advanced countries. In this market we stood the test of three years of public scrutiny and emerged victorious.

I was much happier with this victory than I was when I received word of the "informal decision" the first time around. It was a powerful moment emotionally for me because in the past, while there was always the possibility we might win, it was generally assumed we would be beaten by IBM. What made the victory especially satisfying was the knowledge that, because of the "computer-gate" affair, a completely impartial evaluation was carried out and the true value of Fujitsu computers attested to.

In computer sales it is not just the quality of the hardware that is crucial; software quality is often decisive. Beyond that, it is the system's track record that "speaks loudest." Regardless of the confidence I personally felt, the decision here was being made by another party. On the matter of software record, it was clear that Fujitsu was at a distinct disadvantage vis-à-vis IBM. Nevertheless, what allowed us to overcome this handicap was the fact that the superiority of Fujitsu's OS (basic operating system software) was recognized and appreciated.

Spurred by the success in obtaining the order from the Australian Bureau of Statistics, Fujitsu's international standing rose to a new plateau. By employing the advantages of compatibility, we reached the point where we can now lock horns with IBM right across the field. To do this successfully, it is of utmost importance that Fujitsu's products be "reliable." And in order for this "reliability" to prevail, "creativity" must be fostered by ongoing research. It is this "reliability and creativity" which has become the Fujitsu company motto.

II

ENCOUNTERING COMPUTERS

Participation in the development of the "Capital Defense System" during the war brought home to me the importance of data processing systems and became an underlying cause for my later involvement in the world of computers.

FROM ROWDY KID TO UNIVERSITY STUDENT

Although I am over seventy, I have every intention of continuing with all the verve and vigor I can muster in my present capacity as Chairman of Fujitsu Limited. I, therefore, have little inclination to indulge in reminiscences or premature memoirs. Yet, there is no way I can write a history of Fujitsu without writing about my own career. Both began almost fifty years ago when I was a student in Electrical Engineering at Kyoto Imperial University (at the time Kyoto University was strong in technical fields, in contrast to Tokyo University which raised the best and the brightest in the social sciences).

Early in 1935, shortly before my graduation, encouraged by a professor in my department to give Fuji Electric a try, I took the employment exam, passed, and joined the company. That series of events determined the course of my life which in turn became deeply involved in the fortunes of the company we today call Fujitsu.

At the time, Fuji Electric was preparing to establish a new subsidiary, Fuji Tsushinki (Fuji Telecommunications) to specialize in the production of Siemen's telephone switching equipment. Three months after joining Fuji Electric in June 1935, I was transferred to this new company which was initially capitalized at 3,500,000 yen. In 1967, Fuji Tsushinki changed its name to the present Fujitsu. Having been with the company from the very outset, the history of Fujitsu is also my life history.

I was born during the month of June, 1912, in a small town in a rural section of Hyogo Prefecture. The town, Kamicho, in the county of Taka, was nestled in a valley surrounded by mountains. My father, Iwataro, and mother, Kuma, had eight children: four boys, four girls. I was the seventh born, the third son. At present, only two of my siblings are still alive.

During my childhood I was the leader of the neighborhood gang. I have no recollection of ever staying home and reading a book. Books were something you read at school. After school I'd return home, dump my school bag, and then play outdoors until dark. In spite of these decidedly unstudious habits, my grades were good, and I often sat at the head of my class. I remember that I enjoyed a good prank and from time to time was reprimanded by my teachers.

Although outside I may have been the "pack leader," at home it was a different story. As the seventh of eight children, I often came up with the short end of the stick. My elder brothers had more muscle, and my little brother, being the youngest, was doted upon by my parents. When there were treats to be had, my older brothers with their quick hands would get first pick, and my younger brother would cry and manage to get his with this strategy. My portion was always the smallest. Whether it was because of this or simply through what might be called perseverance, it seemed I developed a good sense of self-reliance. Since I received no special treatment, I had to learn to do things myself. In retrospect, I think, the fact that within the family I had no special position and was merely "the third son" probably had a decisive impact on my life.

My family over four generations operated a local postal service. During the 19th century, subscription mail delivery services began in the small towns and villages of rural areas. The businesses were continued along family lines and later incorporated by the national postal system as "designated post offices."

My father continued the business begun by my grandfather. My elder brother was the third generation and his son is now postmaster of the "designated post office" founded by his great grandfather. Post offices now vie with banks in the range of services they provide but in the early days it was not a fulltime job. By my brother's day it had become a fulltime occupation.

At an early age, my grandfather went into the soy sauce brewing business. He walked around the countryside carrying his barrels, selling soy sauce. The people in the scattered outlying villages often asked him to deliver mail since he was going that way anyway. Thus he became involved in "post office" work. I remember being told all of this as a child.

For the "back country" this was comparatively "advanced" work to be doing, and my father on occasion would obtain information from periodicals on communications sent by the Ministry of Communications. When he learned that something called "wireless communication" had begun, it was evidently quite a shock. He often told us: "This is the end of the age of postal services. From now on it will be the age of communication with electricity. In the countryside, even if you inherit a bit of land, it will be all you can do to barely eke out a living. I will pay for your education until you are on your own two feet, so study hard!" I remember the intensity of his encouragement.

In my father's own case, he so wanted to have the opportunity to study, he had skimmed a bit off the top of the family's soy sauce sales, left home, and traveled to Kyoto. Just after he entered the Third Higher School there, his eldest brother died suddenly. My father was forced to return home and continue the family business. I suppose he felt a certain amount of regret. And it may well be that he wanted to see his dreams somehow fulfilled in me.

I certainly understood my father's feelings, and clearly recall as a child being excited by his aspirations for us. My desire to take the exam to join the Fuji Electric was because of the deep impression my father's ideas had made on me.

When I joined Fuji Electric in 1935, the world was in a depression and employment was hard to come by. Although the competition was stiff, I was fortunate enough to pass the exam. About ten students from the Imperial universities took the examination, but only two were employed.

In the Great Kanto Earthquake of 1923, much of the telephone equipment had been destroyed. The rebuilding which followed coincided with a period of change over to automatic switching. All of the manufacturers in the industry were competing to introduce foreign technology. Fuji Electric also was busily producing knockdowns from Siemen's technology. As I mentioned above, in 1935 a subsidiary company, Fuji Tsushinki (Fuji Telecommunications), the present day Fujitsu, was established especially for this purpose. When I began working at Fujitsu, from dawn to dusk I found myself wearing out dictionaries translating German documentation and technical diagrams. It was a period of high unemployment and when I accepted the job, I said I was willing to do anything—but those were terribly uninteresting days.

My time at the university had been like that too. I was an ambitious kid who had come to the big city determined to succeed, but the various theories my teachers taught me just didn't seem to sink in. There appeared to be no connection between the theories taught in the classroom and the real world. The desire to really make a concerted effort was just not there. My first days at Fujitsu were much the same. When I grumbled my complaints to senior colleagues, they countered with the consolation: "A new company has only blue sky above; the sky is the limit. A blue sky venture may be rough at first, but if you stick with it eventually there are fine rewards."

The thought of quitting presented itself more than once. These feelings were cast aside, however, with the outbreak of the war: The Manchurian Incident, The China Incident, The War in the Pacific. As the world plunged into war, the engineers and scientists now had an opportunity to demonstrate their talents. At least, "the blue sky above" now became a real factor.

WORKING ON THE CAPITAL DEFENSE SYSTEM

The War in the Pacific was set off by the December 8, 1941 attack on Pearl Harbor. The initial phase of the hostilities went well for Japan, but the opposition's military superiority soon put Japan on the defensive. Withdrawal followed withdrawal and before long cities on the Japanese main island of Honshu were under attack. On August 18, 1942, sixteen B25 bombers from the aircraft carrier Hornet raided Tokyo, Yokohama, Nagoya, and Osaka. By 1943, the Japanese mainland was under incessant air attack. Those of us on the home front spent our days watching the skies in order to defend Tokyo from the air raids.

After graduating from the Military Academy and spending a year or two on active duty, engineers who were commissioned officers in the army received a year of general training at the Artillery School. Approximately one third of these men went on to receive special advanced training. Out of this last group, a few with extraordinary promise were selected to enroll at one of the seven imperial universities. During my years at Kyoto Imperial University I remember a number of officers from the army and navy in attendance. They were a very elite group. Later, during the Pacific War, as naval captains and army majors, in such places as the Aviation Technology Headquarters and Military Technology Headquarters, they achieved positions of major importance.

Due to the fact that a classmate of mine was working at The Military Research Institute at Tama in Tokyo, I became involved in the development of a "Capital Defense System." "Capital Defense System" is what we might call the program today. Actually, in 1943 when it originated, I believe the official title was Special Air Defense Project Committee. The project was undertaken to deal with the problems of defending Tokyo—the capital and residence of the Emperor—from enemy bombing. We, for example, were charged with constructing equipment which could, with radio waves, accurately guide our fighters to meet the attacking B29's. By that time, the B29's had already stepped up the frequency of the bombing. Another objective was the development of equipment that could transmit accurate data on the position of enemy aircraft picked up on radar. The data had to be transmitted without any time lapse to anti-aircraft battery positions. The "parallel radio guidance device" was an early application of what we today call data communications technology.

At that time the Japanese Army was in retreat and great quantities of military equipment were being lost and abandoned. Factories all over the country were being requisitioned for munitions production. Thus, under the general mobilization of 1944, Fujitsu Kawasaki factory and others were assigned roles in the war effort by the Military Corporation Act. An annex of the Tama Army Research Institute was set up within our Kawasaki plant.

By then it was no longer possible to construct ferroconcrete buildings. Since there were no supplies of iron or concrete available, new structures had to be built with wood. With controls then in effect, however, even lumber was hard to come by. With no other recourse, we went to an army ordnance post and requested materials in order to conduct "research for the defense of the capital." Eventually we received lumber and cement and managed to construct a two-story, barrack-like building. It was built very quickly and felt almost like a warehouse: the floor boards resounded as you walked through.

There were a number of people assigned to this annex including the late Yosuke Nishimura who later became a Fujitsu engineering manager and board director. I also became a part-time member of the staff at the annex and found myself working harder than ever before. There were no models on which to base our designs, and materials were merely a catalog of unavailables. We had to make each screw and gear needed to conduct our experiments. After a difficult, desperate struggle, the various devices were finally completed. I recall working through the night three days at a stretch.

We succeeded in producing a device which instantaneously transmitted data from radar observations—an anti-aircraft artillery guidance device. The transmitter and signaling device could be broken down and carried by hand. The unfortunate thing was that, although our task was to build a "defense system," we were responsible for only a part of the project. No matter how perfect one part, if the other elements in a system do not work, the system itself is useless. The technical officer directing our group was responsible for only a small part of the enormous military machine; there was little more we could do.

Radar equipment was installed on the top of the Dai-Ichi Mutual Life Insurance Building, at the time the highest in Tokyo, and above the stands of the Korakuen Stadium. Our device was designed to send data picked up on radar to anti-aircraft artillery emplacements and automatically indicate the position of enemy planes to the degree and minute. Up to there, the system was perfect. However, the observation point and the artillery positions were some distance apart, and the rounds fired took about thirty seconds to travel the effective firing range of 7,000 meters. In the interval the B29's would have moved far ahead. Furthermore, without taking into consideration such factors as the ambient temperature and wind velocity, it was impossible to get an accurate fix on future positions. The computation involved just could not be accomplished quickly enough.

During the Second World War, the mechanization and automatization of anti-aircraft artillery guidance systems had advanced extremely rapidly in the U.S. By merely following a remote indicator dial, a gunner could fire his artillery with an electro-mechanical device. That is, "a remote control direct sighting automatic firing method" had been developed. This meant that now observation, calculation, and sighting operations were carried out automatically, and the equipment could deliver a shell which would explode at the required position. As I described above, the system we devised to send the observation data instantaneously to the anti-aircraft units along the Edo River flowing in the eastern part of Tokyo and the Sumidagawa River in the central section worked perfectly. The computation tool which combined a calculator and sighting equipment was, however, a military secret, and we were not permitted to meddle with it.

At one point I had the opportunity to visit one of the anti-aircraft artillery batteries. Although the enemy was using electron tube-based computation devices, our calculations were being done on a mechanical analog machine. It was a piece of equipment manufactured by Army Ordnance which looked like a mass of gears and levers. Toward the very end of the war when machinery and materials were simply not available, handmade wooden parts were used for repairs. I knew that to improve the situation a change had to be made toward electrically powered devices. If relays were used, the computation could be done much more quickly. The air raids were by now, however, being conducted by B29's and there was no time to make the necessary changes. The B29's flew well above the range of the anti-aircraft artillery and rained bombs from the sky. From their perspective it was as though they had come to watch a fireworks display from above. There was now, in fact, no such thing as a "capital defense system."

One officer claimed with an unreasonable show of toughness, "With gravity on our side, we have a very strong ally." But the truth of the matter is that nature is impartial, treating friend and foe alike. At the time, I felt in a vague way, the necessity for what we call today a systems analysis approach with a fast and precise computer at the core.

If I had not had this experience during the war, I wonder if later I would have become as involved with computers as I have. One never knows at the time what will later be recognized as a turning point in one's life. It was then I clearly recognized that the most important or critical question was how to weave together a total system for processing data.

The processes involved in anti-aircraft ballistics were observation, calculation, laying or sighting, and firing. This was essentially a matter of input, computation, and output. I knew that if a fairly large amount of multidimensional data could be organized in a system, it should be possible to process it in various ways. I was confident, however, that this was work for electrical, not mechanical, engineers.

I also felt that things would not go well unless you made your own components. When you are making a device composed of thousands, or tens of thousands of individual parts, unless each of these parts is made with extreme precision and accuracy, you will not be able to get the whole device to work satisfactorily. As the war intensified, because virtually all adult males were sent to fight, condensers and resistors were being made by available civilians, students and cafe waitresses who were mobilized for the task. The situation was such that once when there was talk of inviting the Emperor to view general maneuvers using radio guided equipment, because there was no way of insuring that the radar controlled weapons would operate properly, the whole thing was cancelled. Of course, as it was wartime, there were factors affecting the quality of labor that just could not be helped, but I think, in general, manufacturing methods which call for subcontracting out parts and having the large companies do the assembly are mistaken. I have always felt that the opposite approach was better: well capitalized, large manufacturing companies should invest in producing accurate, high quality parts, and the assembly then be performed by those with more good ideas than capital.

The "Capital Defense System" work, because it was a military project, was not constrained by a tight budget. Money was spent lavishly, and we were able to conduct a variety of experiments. This freedom to pursue what interested me had the marvelous effect of quickly changing what had hitherto been disagreeable work at the company into a very stimulating job. I would take up some task and immediately a problem would arise. While grappling with this problem, I would test even well-known facts to make them my own. I accummulated data and more data. Even if a first appraisal indicated that something was impossible, not content with merely parroting received opinion, I would try it myself. I realized just how important it was to do it this way. This, I understood, was what was meant by seeing "the blue sky above."

The direction my work took after the war, and my approach to this work, was based on this precious experience. The fact, however, that it was obtained during the great tragedy called war, weighs heavily on my mind.

OBSESSED BY COMPUTERS

Before long, the war ended. Naturally, Fujitsu switched back to civilian production and again began manufacturing goods for non-military consumption. However, in order to control the raging postwar inflation, the occupation authorities at General Headquarters (GHQ) instituted a powerful deflationary policy based on the Nine Principles of Economic Stability (which we referred to as "The Dodge Line").

The Japanese economy was hit by a severe recession and the electrical communications industry was no exception. The Ministry of Communications' plans called for a rapid decline in new telephone installations from 140,000 in 1948 to 67,000 in 1949, to 62,000 in 1950. Because of this, beginning with the closing of the Ueda Plant in Nagano Prefecture in 1949, we were forced to reduce our total work force by 36% or 1,492 people. Faced with this situation, the development of new enterprises was our most pressing concern.

As part of the recovery plan, the Japanese government launched a number of new measures in order to nurture and strengthen domestic industries. In December of 1949, the "Industrial Rationalization Review Board" was established. It was charged with:

1. Encouraging modernization and efficiency in industrial plant and equipment.

2. Refurbishing of the infrastructure.

3. Providing assistance for the improvement of the level of production technology.

4. Bolstering the monetary and tax systems, etc. The Board issued reports and generated policy along these lines.

Among the measures taken with respect to science and technology, an Agency of Industrial Science and Technology was set up. Also, the creation of uniform industrial codes was promoted through the establishment of the Japan Industrial Standards (JIS). In 1950, based on the Industrial

Rationalization Promotion Act, a grant fund system was set up to assist experimental research in mining and manufacturing technology. At the same time other subsidy programs for private sector experimental research activities were strengthened. Our company was favored with support from many of these programs.

When this research subsidy system was started, I had just become manager of the Technical Development Department. The manager responsible for our communications with the Ministry of International Trade and Industry (MITI) approached me with a remarkable suggestion. Funds, it seems, were available to promote industrial development. Couldn't we use some? Effective the following year the procedure would be quite different, but, since this was their first fiscal period and budgeted amounts had to be used, our prospects for a grant were excellent. "We don't have enough time," he explained, "to submit a proposal for future research, but if there is anything that looks promising in research projects now underway, why not submit a report?" These days this scenario would be inconceivable, but at that time, very favorable conditions prevailed.

Immediately we prepared and submitted a report on audio standards for telephones and related equipment. We received quick approval and a grant of 300,000 yen. With those funds we purchased a complete set of Articles on Military Technology issued during the Second World War which had been collected by the Massachusetts Institute of Technology. This was to fill in the gaps in our technical information resulting from the war.

Altogether there were perhaps about thirty volumes in the M.I.T. collection. We divided them among ourselves and began reading. It was evident America had been conducting research on a great variety of subjects. From viewing the photos and studying the diagrams, even without a close reading, we obtained a pretty good idea. My immediate response was, "Oh my God, Japan is really behind. It's no wonder we lost the war."

As a result of our research we wrote a memorandum, "The Need to Develop Microwave Multiplex Transmission, Computer, and Television Technologies" which, through the General Manager of our division, was submitted to the board of directors. Compared to Toshiba and NEC, we were behind in microwave technology, and I have already described how computers had become a vision of mine since my involvement in the "capital defense system." Regarding computers in particular, information in the M.I.T. technology articles on the Western Electric Company's relay computer provided great encouragement.

As only a department manager during that period, I had no way of knowing what kind of discussions took place in the board meetings. But one of the directors informed me later that my proposal was given careful consideration.

President Junichi Koh and the directors took my suggestion seriously and visited Siemens, Western Electric and other major corporations to negotiate technology transfer agreements. It is interesting to note that in these discussions television was not given serious consideration.

Various countries were visited, and all kinds of negotiations conducted, but nowhere did we find a willing partner. That is understandable. Japan was in a miserable state—just getting enough to eat was a problem. Foodstuffs were being received through American assistance. We did not appear to be at a level appropriate for introducing something so advanced as television technology. No matter how often we explained that technology like radio and wireless were crucial for developing communications and industry, they refused to deal with us. Within the company, and in our parent company Fuji Electric as well, the same mood prevailed—accept the fact that it is a bitter thing to be a defeated country. Had we used the expression "image transmission" (using Japanese characters) instead of the foreign term *terebi* (television), it might have been easier to move the internal discussion forward, but that's merely Monday morning quarterbacking.

This is not to say, by the way, it would have been better for Fujitsu to have concentrated on television technology. This is a product which intrinsically our parent company Fuji Electric ought to have handled. Actually, sometime later, they did begin producing television equipment but their timing was really off. If it was going to be done at all, it should have been taken up when Fujitsu first raised the possibility. If that had been the case, the structure of today's consumer electronics industry would probably be quite different. Unless you have a great deal of strength the only way to succeed is to get a jump on everyone else and quickly build experience and a track record. Because Hitachi had strength, even though they got into television late, they caught up beautifully.

As for microwave radio, in 1952, as a consequence of old ties, technical cooperation with Siemens A.G. was revived. The following year a technical assistance agreement was concluded in the area of components. Although Siemens certainly does fine work, they too were on the losing side of the war and were not able to devote so much to research and development. For this reason we knew we could not totally rely on Siemens: The only way was to do it ourselves. As a result, the technical specialists in Fujitsu were roused into activity. Their engineering spirit was invigorated. Over the long run I think this turned out to be a tremendous benefit.

Japanese companies, in order to raise their level of manufacturing technology which had fallen behind their counterparts in the advanced nations of Europe and North America, were competing to introduce new technologies from abroad. I thought that it would be better, if at all possible, to do what we could with our own abilities. This might sound incredibly self-confident, but the truth of the matter is, depending on some other party for detailed technical information involves grave risks. Published data is only data from a particular set of circumstances and conditions. Actual phenomena are never so simple as to permit expression with a single set of figures. To believe the figures, to swallow them whole, can lead you to commit grievous mistakes.

From observing those around me, it appears that when Fujitsu people read a book, they do not generally read from cover to cover trying to memorize every little detail. Ideas and inspirations are what are obtained from books, not data. The general feeling seems to be that data is something you produce yourself. It seems to me, it was during those early days that this propensity to "do it myself" arose at Fujitsu, and I believe it has become the source of the "fight" in the Fujitsu man.

Of the three main topics dealt with in my proposal, in the area of computers we were not able to obtain technology agreements with anyone. Consequently, we had to do all of the development ourselves. Looking back, I would have to say we were surprisingly lucky in this endeavor which promised to be one uphill struggle after another with tremendous obstacles along the way. Fujitsu had a streak of good fortune that greatly facilitated our move into computer technology.

The first and foremost was the existence of Toshio Ikeda. A graduate of Tokyo Institute of Technology, he joined

Fujitsu and designed our first computer, the FACOM 100. It has been said that if it were not for him, there would not have been a Fujitsu computer. Ikeda possessed a rare genius for computer development. Not infrequently, when an idea occurred to him, he would work through the night. Beginning with the relay style statistics tabulator, which was developed for the Tokyo Metropolitan Government, he put everything into the development of Fujitsu computers. To my regret, in 1974, (then a board director) while still a young man, he died suddenly.

Next, there was Shinsuke Shiokawa. As early as 1938, he had attracted attention when he delivered a paper on binary computation with electronic circuits at an academic conference. He went to work for Fuji Electric and during the war years developed a "Digital Four Function Electric Abacus." Shiokawa left Fuji Electric in 1945, but in 1951 he was offered and accepted a position with Fujitsu.

The third individual to whom we owe so much is Professor Hideo Yamashita of Tokyo University. Professor Yamashita, an early proponent of Shiokawa's digital approach, spent the years from 1940 to 1947 completing a sorting and tabulating machine. Work on the Statistics Tabulator for the Tokyo Metropolitan Government mentioned previously was initiated by a request from the professor.

In 1952 Professor Yamashita sounded me out: "Any interest in doing a stock transfer and accounting system for the Tokyo Stock Exchange?" Having been thinking about computers since the war and being at that time manager of research and development, I responded immediately: "We'd like to do it." We were fortunate again in that my boss, Hanzo Omi, the General Manager for Engineering, was of the opinion that Fujitsu, as a manufacturer of communication equipment, should also be active in the field of calculation and computation devices.

So with Ikeda as a leader, a team was created which included Takuma Yamamoto, now president of Fujitsu, Ltd., Shoki Yamaguchi, Shiokawa, and others. A few months later we were ready to put the finishing touches on the completed system. It turned out, however, that this model was never actually used by the Stock Exchange. Instead, some time later this Stock Transaction Computation System which used over 10,000 relays was installed and put into operation at Daiwa Securities. A dividend of this project was that Ikeda was now totally captivated by computers.

THE BIRTH OF FACOM

The Stock Transaction Computation System was developed to counter the punch card systems (PCS) of IBM and Univac. It was a challenge which represented our refusal to accept the power of established giants in the field. Our system utilized paper tape for input. While it had some distinct advantages, for the sorting operations so very important for business calculations, it did not work well. First of all, the sorting speed was slower than the punch card system. Second, our paper tape system was subject to too many breakdowns. On a number of occasions, General Manager Omi and I found ourselves hastening to the site of planned demonstrations on the very morning customers were expected after being advised that the system was not functioning properly. Faced with this lack of dependability, it was decided that it would be better to shift our research emphasis to systems for scientific applications. Science and engineering problems usually required extended processing of limited amounts of data. The direction of our research and development effort was adjusted accordingly.

Toshio Ikeda used to tell a story about the time he went to the theater with the company president Ko to see a performance by the Soviet Ballet. Taking advantage of the president's total absorption in the ballerinas, Ikeda got him to agree to proceed with computer development. Of course, I have no way of confirming the truth of this story but Ikeda may well have done so since there is no doubt that he wanted very much to move ahead with computer research.

There are numerous stories about Ikeda. One time a fire broke out in the factory where a prototype machine was being tested. Thinking that if the schematic diagrams with all of the designs were burned, they would have to begin again from scratch, his subordinates were about to dash into the fire to save them. Up ran Ikeda to the site of the fire yelling, "Stay away. It's dangerous. If you're worried about the plans, they're all here in my head." He did, in fact, reconstruct the lost plans. This is one of the "legends" that have been passed down about him.

Ikeda's genius and efforts were truly outstanding. At the same time, his work habits too were rather unusual. He would work at home refining an idea during the day, and eventually toward evening appear at the office. There were complaints within the company about not adhering to company policy, and as supervisor I was put in a difficult position. Without his incomparable talents, our work could not have advanced. At the time, Fujitsu's payroll was calculated on a daily basis. As a result there were times when Ikeda did not receive satisfactory compensation. Since this was not very fair, I conferred with Omi and arranged for Ikeda to be paid on a monthly basis. It was a strange state of affairs: More than once I was awakened at home in the middle of the night when Ikeda arrived with something he had to talk over that just could not wait.

In any event, a project team of "curious" individuals was assembled (it grew to about ten people) and, if nothing else, the enthusiasm was tremendous. Eighteen months later, in the fall of 1954, they completed the first Fujitsu Electric Computer FD1. It used relays for the processing, memory, and control section. Since telephone switching relays could not be used as they were, everything, down to the relay, was newly designed and produced.

The FD1 was a temporary designation. Omi, Fujitsu Engineering Manager, later officially named the machine, FACOM 100—for *Fu*ji *A*utomatic *Com*puter. As I mentioned above, the bulk of the money we had available for this project came from the MITI subsidy program for mining and industrial research. We were still being treated like a stepchild by Fujitsu and consequently received very little in the way of a development budget.

The completed FACOM 100 was intended to be used for scientific computation. We did some computations on it at the request of universities and industry free of charge. One of the requests received was from Dr. Hideki Yukawa, a Nobel Prize winner in physics from Kyoto University, for a complex integral calculus computation. He was extremely pleased with the results. The calculation, which if done by a human being would have taken two years, was accomplished in only three days.

The next to be developed were Japan's first computers for business applications: The FACOM 128A and 128B. These models at first glance look very much like telephone switching equipment, but are said to be "masterpieces" of early relay style computers. The 128B is now still functioning beautifully in the Ikeda Memorial Room of Fujitsu's Numazu Factory.

III

CHALLENGE

With President Okada at the helm, Fujitsu stakes its future on computers. Plans to introduce IBM technology fall through and we struggle with the problems of independent development.

BRINGING HOME A "STRAY"

During the latter half of the 1950's and into the 1960's, Japan's economy witnessed the end of a period of reconstruction and the beginnings of industrial independence.

The Korean War which broke out in June 1950, stimulated a boom in demand and put new energy into the economy which, up to then, due to the Dodge line policy, had been fitful and sluggish. As businesses actively invested in new plant and equipment and obsolete facilities were modernized, Japan's international competitive posture was gradually strengthened. By the beginning of the 1960's, increasing demands for Japan to open up its domestic markets began to be heard from various countries. In response to this pressure, slow but deliberate steps were taken to liberalize trade policies. In 1960, the outline of a plan to liberalize foreign currency exchange laws was drawn up. Three years later, sweeping changes in currency exchange regulations were announced. In 1964, Japan became a participant in the International Monetary Fund and joined the OECD.

It was in this economic environment that our drive to become a viable computer manufacturer got underway. Although for the sake of independent development our computer engineers literally forgot about food and sleep in their effort to forge ahead, the fruit of these labors was not at first readily apparent. At one point we imported card readers and other peripherals from IBM and connected them to Fujitsu computers. This did not work out as well as we thought it might for two reasons: First, our contract with IBM left us practically no margin; and second, the only input/output card devices made available to us were older models.

It was about that time that I became responsible for radio transmission systems, one of the areas of major concern just after the war. Microwave transmission equipment had been developed, and I made the rounds making sales calls on electric utilities, etc. I became deeply involved in sales and for three years, from 1957-1960, served as Director of our Osaka sales office. During my time in both Tokyo and Osaka, I think about thirty relay style computers were sold.

Fujitsu computers at that time had a unique architecture. Because other computers had a relatively low reliability level, it was necessary for them to process the same data twice in order to check for errors. We, on the other hand, considered computation speed important, but thought the elimination of machine error was even more important. To achieve this, a special processor was used to check the CPU and insure that the right answer was obtained the first time. The processing power was doubled, but at the same time, the price went up 10 to 20%.

When I was in Osaka, I approached Kansai Electric Power Company about the possibility of buying the computer being built by our computer group in Tokyo. They agreed to purchase the machine and made plans accordingly. Even after considerable delay, however, the computer, now a critical element in their plans, was still not ready for delivery. I phoned many times to urge Tokyo to speed things up. Finally, Ikeda (then Computer Department Manager) and a number of others made the trip to Osaka. They asked that I return with them to the factory and lend a hand. Asked why, they responded that they had become involved with a variety of different computers and had almost lost control of the situation at the production facilities. They believed some consolidation of the various models was necessary and wanted me to bring my experience to bear on the problem.

I visited the factory, as requested, and found it to be much the same as five or six years before. It was just as if a number of stray kittens had been brought home and deemed so cute they were all kept around as pets. Like ants swarming over cake, in every nook and cranny of the Kawasaki Factory, people were busy working. Observing carefully, I could see there were the original relay style computers, three types of parametron computers, and a large transistor mainframe. Each pocket of activity went about its work, but when asked when one of them would be finished, or how far along they were, nobody knew. No matter how you looked at this way of doing things, it could not be called "industrial manufacturing."

After examining the situation from different perspectives, it was decided that the parametron projects be halted. We had already, however, received orders for this particular type system from Kansai Electric Power Co. and could not very well cancel them. So we resolved to proceed as planned and fulfill existing contracts but not accept any further orders for parametron-type computers. Our activities became focused on getting the transistor mainframe–the FACOM 222–ready to market. Since it was also clear that manufacturing computers in a wing of a factory devoted to communications equipment was not the best way to push forward with our computer development, our next concern became the construction of a specialized facility for computer manufacturing.

This was the state of affairs in Fujitsu's computer department until about 1960: It was a bunch of crazy, exhuberant engineers without any overall organization. In my position as Radio Transmission Systems Department Manager and as Assistant Head of the Sales Department, for five or six years I had worked in a sales capacity. I had first-hand knowledge of how customers use our machines and had a strong sense of how important timely delivery is. I was confident the market for computers would grow. But I also knew, from here on out, that simply gathering a diversified crew of "eccentric" engineers was not the way; first and foremost on the agenda was the establishment of an internal structure to deal with computers.

THE CHALLENGE

With this in mind, at a meeting of our National Conference of Regional Sales Office Managers, I presented the following rather audacious proposal to Tsunesuke Wada, then company President. "In the computer field, our company is five years ahead of our competitors in Japan. The technology we have accumulated makes the prospect of another company overtaking us very unlikely no matter what contortions they might perform. Whether the elements are relays or transistors, the fundamentals do not change. Since there is no doubt computers will become a large market in the future, it is essential that our company be organized to meet that challenge. To fail to do so would be irresponsible to our customers."

At that time, the various managers responsible for different areas in sales, engineering, and manufacturing each proceeded in their own manner, and it was not possible to have a quick overall response to a pressing need. It was, therefore, necessary to pull everything together into a more responsive corporate structure. This was easier said than done. What we were proposing was not only a move into completely unknown territory, but we did not even have the personnel who could bring to the problems a comprehensive command of the situation. When President Wada raised this question at the meeting, saying, "We don't have anyone who can handle the job, do we?" I found myself replying, "If there is no one else, why don't I do it?"

I suppose we can attribute my response to the fact that I was still young, sanguine, and full of vigor. In any event, it was thus that the Electronics Department was born in Fujitsu, and I returned to Tokyo as head of the department to grapple with the problems of computer development. I plunged head first into the construction of a new factory—my first priority. At the time, I was wearing two hats: my other position being Assistant Manager for Engineering. The head of engineering then was Hiroshi Seimiya, my predecessor as President of Fujitsu Limited.

Since we were trying to run things along new corporate division lines, I also had to keep an eye on developments in each of our business lines. One of my first considerations was how to deal with orders which had already been received. Specifically, we had outstanding orders from the Tokyo University School of Physical Sciences (H. Takahashi Research Laboratory), the Industrial Science Institute of Tokyo University, and Toyota Motor Corp. The orders were for a new generation, epoch-making, large scale computer, the Parametron PC2 (FACOM 202). In addition, we had been entrusted with the manufacture of the Musashino No. 1 (FACOM 201) for the Research Institute of Nippon Telegraph and Telephone.

We could not very well cancel all of these orders. Yet significant problems with the Parametron PC2 were still to be resolved. When the order for the Parametron PC2 was received from Toyota, I can remember ripples of anger surfacing in the company. The reason for this was that some of the components of the system failed to function properly. The parametron was Fujitsu's first practical commercial computer; about thirty were eventually produced making it a best-seller at the time.

The machine's electrical power consumption was high however, and it generated a tremendous amount of heat. Consequently, not only did the cost of cooling equipment become excessive, but the oil that was used as a coolant would sometimes leak from odd places.

Despite these difficulties, it would have been irresponsible to tell these very important customers that we had discontinued the parametron. So we responded by installing the computers as ordered and then meeting with the users to advise them, "Henceforth, it will be transistors. Please use this system we have provided and give your every consideration to the models which will be forthcoming." Those users are still valuable Fujitsu customers today.

Soon after I returned to the head office in Tokyo, I heard that Kanjiro Okada would be asked to assume the position of President. It was a marvelous surprise. More than a surprise, I was so pleased I felt it was a wonderful god-send. Before the war, Okada had been President of Furukawa Co. He was ousted in a realignment, and later moved to Ube Industries (Cement Company) where he rose to the position of Executive Vice President. He had retired from his post and moved to the Shonan coast where he planned to spend a quiet retirement with his wife. Wada, who was serving as President of both Fuji Electric and Fujitsu, approached him with the request that he take over his responsibilities as Fujitsu President. This led to Okada finally assuming the position toward the end of 1959.

My joy at this turn of events was not due only to the fact that Fujitsu would now have such a prominent and distinguished President. Some years earlier, in 1955 when I had just moved into operations, Shiokawa and I called on Okada at Ube Industries to discuss computers. My impression was one of a calm gentleman, with a quick mind who seemed to be a repository of wisdom. What excited me was that Okada had listened to our presentation, nodding from time to time as if in agreement, and had shown a great enthusiasm for computers. I thought he would understand and empathize with our plans. In order to launch a major effort in the computer field, President Wada had probably sought to persuade a prominent figure with an understanding of computers to take charge.

President Wada appears to have told the newly appointed Okada about my persistance at our national sales conference. Because right after the new President gave his inaugural address, he said to me, "You're Kobayashi, aren't you? Give it your best."

They were just a few words, but I took heart in the warm encouragement. Since then, in every area right across the board, I have been profoundly influenced by Okada. I was able to say what I thought and given the go-ahead to do what needed to be done.

Throughout my life I have received kind instruction and direction from many of my senior colleagues, but among them, the one who made the deepest impression was Okada. He not only had a firm, clear vision of the future, his eye for people was equally sharp. Time after time while taking the lead in moving forward, he avoided becoming personally involved in this move or that. He made it appear that it was left to everyone's own initiative. While everyone felt they were pursuing their freely chosen objectives, Okada was carefully moving everything in his own targeted direction. What a rich experience it was to have been able to study his management style.

CONSTRUCTION OF A SPECIALIZED FACTORY

With empathy and understanding at the top, those of us in the ranks really began to hustle. Our first order of business was a plan to construct a new factory devoted to computers. I was to devise the plan and present it to the Board of Directors. President Okada aside, most of the directors as yet had no understanding of computers. Regardless of the merits of our plan, because we were still viewed with the bias accorded a stepchild, we could expect a predictably sour response.

My plan called for constructing the building in two phases. During the first phase, half of the facility would be built. In the middle of my presentation, President Okada interrupted and asked, "Why not build a large one from the beginning?" Despite the fact that many of us on the planning committee had our doubts about whether such a huge plant, if built, would be fully utilized, Okada's prescience was remarkable. One year after the new factory was completed, in November 1961, it was operating at full capacity.

As might be expected, more than half of the directors preferred a more cautious course of action which dealt with known quantities. Rather than attempting some unknown, untried X or Y, if we stuck to contract work for Nippon Telegraph and Telephone, it had the advantages a long and steady relationship offers, as well as the prospect of assured profitability. Okada, however, having come from outside and having had the opportunity to take a long hard look at contemporary trends, had a strong belief in the future of the market for computers. Our group could not have asked for stronger leadership.

Okada disregarded the advice of the directors set in their old ways. He quickly picked a number of young men like our computer group and assigned them to important positions in the company. Although it was a radical recasting of the company, I do not think our business could have been transformed so quickly had he not done so. Mass media at the time pretty much ignored this aspect of the changes. From the point of view of the people directly involved it was strong medicine and only possible because of Okada.

WITHOUT THE INTRODUCTION OF FOREIGN TECHNOLOGY

Fujitsu was now clearly committed to computers. Like many other Japanese businesses at the time, we gave serious consideration to introducing advanced European and American technology. It was, of course, the easiest method of obtaining such technology. In the computer field, agreements had already been signed with strong foreign companies: Toshiba with GE, Hitachi with RCA, NEC with Honeywell, and Oki Electric with Univac. It seemed natural enough then that our partner would be the computer giant,

IBM. This was in 1961. It turned out, however, that when negotiations to introduce IBM technology were conducted, IBM flatly refused to consider technology transfers unless they were given 100% capital participation. This was "IBM's world policy." Of course, there was no way that Fujitsu was going to become a wholly owned subsidiary of IBM. This meant that independent development was now the only route open. And although that path was not an easy one, to be sure, I think it fair to say our hard work is bearing fruit today.

As I have already mentioned, Nippon Telegraph and Telephone is one of Fujitsu's main customers—primarily for telephone switching equipment. We also have tried to sell them computers. As a public monopoly business, however, they had an unwritten policy that worked against us: Regardless of how hard we strove, as a manufacturer late to the market we were not able to displace NEC which was there first. A friend of mine at Nippon Telegraph and Telephone told me, "If you want to obtain a lion's share of the orders from us, you have to become the undisputed leader so well known in markets outside NTT's sphere of influence, that everyone will be asking why we are not buying Fujitsu equipment." This bit of "advice" served only to strengthen my determination and whet my appetite for future competition.

Although somewhat later, our experience with the Tokyo Stock Exchange was similar. Fujitsu was first to develop an experimental model, but Hitachi made the first sale and totally controlled things thereafter. However, when Fujitsu became number one in computers in Japan, a managing director of the Exchange, approached us directly: "For the Exchange, which is a public institution, to have absolutely no business with Fujitsu is not right. I ask for your cooperation in rectifying this situation." We were very happy to hear this proposal and, needless to say, took advantage of the opportunity. Nonetheless, it is clear that developing real capability and technological leadership are the primary factors in business growth.

President Okada staked the future of Fujitsu on computers. During his ten years at the helm, he completely changed the atmosphere and business posture of the company. Kora and Seimiya followed and fifteen years later, I found myself in the same position as company President. I merely proceeded to put into effect what I had been taught during those ten years. For example, in the case of a new business undertaking, if three of the ten directors were in agreement, it was "go ahead"; if five agreed, it was "too late." By the time half agreed, it was usually already too late in the game to be successful.

I differed with Okada's management style on only one point. He was very enthusiastic about centralized administration and had a negative view of the value of decentralized operations. Okada had a great deal of confidence and strength, and thus seemed to feel that centralized control was the most effective approach. For someone like myself without that great strength, I decided it would work better if I decentralized operations and delegated authority to individuals responsible for various areas.

After Okada retired, the process of decentralization began under President Kora. Subsidiaries such as FANUC (a company specializing in robotics and numerically controlled machinery) were established one after another and a large Fujitsu Group began to take shape. In retrospect, I think the decentralization policy has been successful.

JUST LIKE "FAMILY TIES"

Fujitsu today has become Japan's premier computer manufacturer. During the early 60's, however, we were regarded as being in third place trailing in the dust left behind by Hitachi and NEC. By 1968, Fujitsu had surpassed both, and become the top domestic computer company. During that decade there was considerable debate over just whether a domestic computer industry was really feasible. Due to the fact that computers are very expensive items, users were not able to invest the huge sums required all at once. Because rapid technological advancement in the field encouraged the leasing rather than purchasing of computer equipment, a large percentage of the business was done on a rental basis. Although manufacturers incurred large development and marketing expenses, because income was dependent on rentals, their cash flow problems became more severe the more computers they sold. In order to secure future market share, companies were forced to offer equipment at special discount prices. Naturally profits were being squeezed and finances were strained. Given these circumstances, every company in the field was constantly faced with the problem of whether to proceed or abandon their efforts.

This is the situation which, in August 1961, prompted the establishment of the Japan Electronic Computer Company (JECC) with pooled funds from a consortium of the seven Japanese computer manufactures. JECC was set up to take over the finance function by executing rental agreements with the users. Computers could then be sold to JECC, expenses recovered, and accompanying profits flow in. In other words, the JECC rental system was a way of advancing the time frame for profit accumulation, and greatly reducing the capital requirements of the manufacturers. There were, nevertheless, problems with this arrangement too. If the customer used the equipment for three to four years, the computers would be pretty much paid off and even if the rental was discontinued, this would not cause any problems. If, however, the user were to cancel the contract after a short period (which by the terms of the agreement they were permitted to do after a term of one year and a three month grace period), then the manufacturer had to repurchase the equipment from JECC at a price equivalent to the original sale price less depreciation. In this case the computer companies, which had realized a profit from their sales and already paid taxes on these gains, were forced to buy back the same equipment at high book value. These cancelled rentals and buy-backs became a tremendous burden on the industry.

If a product developed a bad reputation, or if a competitor came out with a new model, contracts were likely to be quickly cancelled. A series of such occurrences could have brought on a financial crisis and threatened the future of the entire computer industry in Japan.

As if top management did not have enough headaches, from time to time the president of one of the industry leaders appears to have stated at meetings with major stockholders that "in order to preserve the financial well being of our company, we plan to keep our computer sales to a level of 25 to 26 percent of total revenues." This was reported in the newspapers and immediately reflected in the market.

Fujitsu, on the other hand, held firmly to President Okada's course. He continued to maintain that, "Fujitsu has staked its future on computers." From the customer's point of view, this was reassuring: "Unlike a company which is ready to pull out of the business as soon as they think profitability is threatened, Fujitsu is sticking with it and is likely to look after our needs well into the future." It became easier to do business with customers like this because of the stand Fujitsu had taken.

To use a baseball metaphor, it is not as though we scored by hitting a home run; we won due to our opponents' errors—never, of course, the best way to win. Just a few words from top management had a tremendous impact. It was a lesson demonstrating the necessity for executives to exercise caution and discretion in their public statements.

In another instance, a different company, caught up in the intensifying competition, became involved in a bribery incident with a government official and was forced to suspend all transactions with government agencies. Here, too, Fujitsu was able to take advantage of the opening and expand our business in this area. In short, because the computer business is profoundly affected by "company image," and is not a one unit here, one unit there, deal-by-deal type of business, the maintenance of "family ties" developed over long periods of interaction is extremely important. If the company "image," however, suffers a severe blow, there is a chain reaction, severing ties right down the line.

Fortunately, due to the fact that Fujitsu made no major errors in this regard, before long we found our hand being raised in the center of the ring.

In 1979, Fujitsu replaced IBM Japan, which for a long time had been number one in our country, as the largest computer vender in Japan. Here, too, it was more a matter of IBM Japan's sluggish growth, than a sudden surge in Fujitsu's sales. I am not sure what caused the slow down at IBM Japan. But if I were to venture an explanation, I would say the source of the problem was in human resource policy.

A common managerial response to the oil shock and subsequent downturn was to cut back in the area of hiring new personnel. Even IBM Japan took such measures. Believing, as I do, that in the computer field, the customer's greatest concern is for full system support, we did not reduce our hiring levels. It is this perhaps, that made the difference.

SUCCESSFUL SALE TO KYOTO UNIVERSITY

The product which marked the beginning of a new epoch for Fujitsu was the integrated circuit computer, FACOM 230-60, introduced in 1965. We had complete confidence in it and independent evaluations gave it high marks. In a sense, it might be said that the FACOM 230-60 was a strategic turning point.

At that time, universities were the most important customers among mainframe computer users. The Fujitsu 230-60 had not yet been completed when Tokyo University installed a Hitachi 5020 built with technology from RCA. To make up for this humiliation at Tokyo University, we concentrated our efforts on Kyoto University with whom we had already initiated discussions. If we were to fail here, there was the real possibility that we would be forced to withdraw from the field of computer manufacturers. We truly had our backs to the wall.

We approached Kyoto University with a request to use our system even though we had not yet completed the design nor were we even able to provide a clear indication of the final form. An audacious position, no doubt, but fortunately they agreed to our proposals. A mid-sized computer, the 230-50, was used for simulation to produce the 230-60. In other words, this was an instance of a computer being used to design a more advanced computer—another watershed for Fujitsu.

Why, you may ask, did Kyoto University agree to use our computer when it was still on the drawing board? I think there was probably some underlying rivalry with Tokyo University at work here. At the same time, there must have also been the desire to cooperate with Fujitsu and contribute their own efforts because it was Japanese, not foreign technology, behind our computer. The professors rallied to the cause. One, responding to our explanation, exclaimed, "It will be an incredible machine. We'll do more than use it; we want to have the world applauding in admiration." The 230-60 not only had the virtue of being domestic technology, but it was the first to employ a state-of-the-art operating system, and Tokyo University had nothing like its advanced multi-processor architecture. The University faculty had great expectations for their system with dual processors which, although it did not double the processing capability, increased it by a factor of 1.7.

NEC was then first among computer manufacturers and Hitachi second. But both were producing systems based on foreign technology. We trailed in third place with our independently developed technology. When negotiations were held with Kyoto University, I joined Ikeda on the sales calls. From the outset we were prepared for a hard struggle. The fact of the matter was that Kyoto University had until then been using a Hitachi system and when it came to an upgrading of the University's computer facilities, Hitachi had a distinct advantage.

I remember rising early many mornings to catch the bullet train and make the trip to Kyoto from Tokyo. On occasion, we would arrive at the Miyako Hotel near the university and run into salesmen from rival companies, there for the same purpose as we. Since there were Kyoto University alumi like myself from other companies who were using their network of associations to help their sales effort, I encountered friends from my college days. We joked and kidded with each other outwardly, but inside each was fiercely determined to "bring home this order."

The reason, incidentally, we were using the Miyako Hotel lobby for meetings was because in Japan, as elsewhere around the world, the student protest movement of the 1960's was at its peak. The Kyoto University campus was in an uproar and the faculty was staying away from the school. Having no other recourse, we had to conduct these discussions off-campus. Fujitsu at that time did not have an office in Kyoto, so we met in the hotel lobby which could be freely used.

The words "student protest" call to mind the steel plates which covered the "windows" of the computer center housing the university's computers. They were supposed to withstand rocks thrown by students from outside. Thinking back, I realize it was a truly brutal scene.

Shortly after this came the episode at Kyushu University. Just before we were about to install a computer system there, by a stroke of bad luck, an American Phantom fighter jet crashed into the computer center and hung suspended from a concrete wall. The incident so stirred up the students, then still engaged in campus protest activities, that work to remove the wrecked plane could not proceed. Consequently, there was no place to install the computer ready for delivery. It was put on the back burner for a while, but since we could not do so indefinitely, we gave up waiting for the reconstruction of the computer center and installed the equipment temporarily in the Kyushu Electric Power Company's gymnasium.

Meanwhile at Kyoto University the professors who were all so knowledgeable about computers, enthusiastically offered their assistance on everything from basic design to the creation of an operating system. Because the 230-60 was a computer made with another computer they were convinced that the performance would be exactly as predicted by our calculations. Since for us, however, this was our first experience with this type of system, a tinge of anxiety could not be dispelled. Despite what theory indicated should be the case, we were not entirely certain of the reliability level.

To meet any contingency, President Okada gathered together hand-picked employees and organized them into special units. The major problem was the introduction of integrated circuits and the production of the printed circuit boards they were mounted on. This was the first attempt to convert the previously used method of soldering copper wiring for circuitry to full use of printed circuit boards. This involved multi-layered boards which were stacked and drilled with holes. The inside of the holes then had to be metal-plated. We had not yet, however, perfected the engineering technology of plating the inner edges of these holes. Thus a special task force was set up in our research laboratory with groups to study new manufacturing techniques to solve problems such as this and work on the operating system.

Almost every month, it seemed, university faculty members would appear at the Kawasaki Factory to exchange opinions and check on our progress. Thanks to the professors' constant attention and involvement until the system was up and running, we managed to complete the computer on schedule.

Although the computer was completed, the necessary software was still inadequate, and we were not able to deliver the efficiency we had promised. I am afraid this caused a certain amount of trouble. The main reason for these difficulties was that the operating system was not performing up to expectations. It was about six months after the computer was installed, I believe, when Professor Tojiro Ishihara, the Director of the Kyoto University Computer Center, came to deliver a formal complaint to the Fujitsu President. Professor Ishihara was a professor of civil engineering, with perhaps a dash of the heroic about him. In any case, he had a large build and was certainly intimidating.

One might tend to think there is little connection between civil engineering and computers, but a bit of background here will help to explain. During that period the civil engineering departments at universities were having trouble attracting superior students. All the better candidates were going into electrical engineering and related fields. Professor Ishihara was disturbed by this and surprised to learn during a trip to M.I.T. in the United States that the civil engineering students there were all very able and motivated, and the department enjoyed a great deal of popularity. Further inquiry revealed that the use of computers at M.I.T. to develop new civil engineering technology had had an invigorating effect on the discipline. Inspired by this, Professor Ishihara, upon returning to Japan, became the driving force behind a campaign to introduce computers into the Kyoto University Civil Engineering Department.

In any event, when Professor Ishihara entered the President's office, I did my best to hide in the shadow of the President. The professor had no sooner settled onto the sofa, than he broke the ice with his deep voice, "You reduced the price by whatever it was, and we paid you exactly as agreed. But, the performance your machine delivered amounts to an absolute breach of the agreement. Why it is practically fraud!" We could only respond, "We thoroughly understand your anger, but ask that you kindly extend us a little more time."

We managed to "escape" that time but later it was worse. The crux of the problem was that our independent development entailed unavoidable delays. Software development, for example, was treated with a "human wave strategy" and having a large number of people working on a project led to communication gaps and inevitable delays. Among other problems, there were for instance three line printers at Kyoto University but we could only get one to work.

Nevertheless, thanks to many hours of hard work, one year later things were so much better Professor Ishihara visited us to extend his thanks "for a job very well done."

Subsequently, a well known American consulting firm evaluated the operating system we had developed. They gave it a very high rating, and Fujitsu's standing moved up a notch.

Due to our success at Kyoto University, the 230-60 was installed at three more of the seven major national universities—in addition to Kyoto, Kyushu, Nagoya and Hokkaido Universities. Thanks also to this success in the academic market, financial institutions and other important users began to use our systems. There was a sense in the air that Fujitsu's mainframe computers were now dominant and this became a topic of discussion throughout the country.

To be sure, the computers sold to the universities were sold at minimal prices, and while there was honor, there was not much in the way of profits. More important, however, was the fact that once they were in the universities, the students became interested, the number of people who wanted to pursue careers in computers increased, and many of them joined Fujitsu. This was a benefit money could not buy.

In addition to the universities, NTT, Dai-Ichi Bank (now Dai-Ichi Kangyo Bank), and a nationwide network of savings banks, one after another, began using Fujitsu computers. We had emerged as the top domestic computer company.

IV

RELIABILITY AND CREATIVITY

An "unlimited liability agreement" for a totalizator sparks the beginning of a reliability campaign. Reliability and creativity becomes the Fujitsu motto.

THE INSIDE TRACK TO QUALITY

Accepting the challenge of "unlimited liability" throughout its nearly fifty year history, Fujitsu has consistently remained faithful to the ideas of reliability and creativity. One instance of this which I will never forget is the computer system sold to the Japan Racing Association. A clause committing us to unlimited liability was incorporated into the contract.

Several years ago, there was an incident reported involving the overpayment of one hundred and twenty million yen in winnings at the Toride Race Track in Ibaraki Prefecture. According to newspaper accounts, the computation error only became evident after the computer had calculated the payoffs on one-fourth of the winning bicycle race tickets, and it was discovered there were not enough funds to make the payments. The President of the company responsible for the tabulation, computation and maintenance of the computer at this race track said, "Until recently only the tabulation of revenues was done on the computer. The calculation of winning bets was a manual operation. Three months ago we switched over to processing both on the computer and rewrote the program. It appears the program had a bug in it."

Even after they caught the computational error, they knew that if they tried to suspend payouts, the fans would go crazy and they would have serious trouble. So it seems they were forced to continue the overpayments. The patrons could not be appeased any other way. There was simply no substitute for money. I sympathized with their no-win situation. The news was of more than passing interest to me because Fujitsu had delivered a computer system to a race track called "Gambling King" which was for just this kind of calculation and computation.

Fujitsu's relationship with the Japan Racing Association has a long history going back to 1935, the year I joined the company. On the governing board of the Racing Association was a scientist with a Ph.D who, beginning with the starting gate apparatus, was enthusiastically mechanizing all he could. Unlike today, the race track in those days was a social gathering place for gentlemen and ladies with a sporting streak. No one was permitted in the first class boxes unless they were wearing formal kimono or western style attire. Even so, because money was involved, a computation error was unacceptable.

Anyway, the racing association scientist was interested in developing an electrical system that would quickly inform the spectators of the total number of bets placed, the odds, payoffs and final results—what today is a commonplace electronic display board. One of his classmates from college was with Fujitsu and the request to research the feasibility of such a system grew out of this connection.

During and right after the war, racetracks had, of course, been closed due to the lack of resources and funds. Research on a suitable system resumed in 1950. By 1956, a prototype totalizator was completed which used the telephone switching relays Fujitsu was justifiably proud of. The following year the first totalizator in Japan was installed at the Nakayama Race Track.

Later, this totalizator was converted from relays to an electronic system and by 1965, the processing was being performed by a computer. The contract with the Central Horse Racing Association we signed on this occasion was truly epoch making: "Fujitsu has invested time and energy over a long period, cooperating with us in the development of this system. We have not contributed any money. Therefore, we want to order exclusively from Fujitsu. However, because our association is under the jurisdiction of the Ministry of Agriculture, Forestry and Fishery, in order to establish an exclusive contract we have to have terms and conditions which will satisfy the Ministry of Finance and the government's Audit Bureau. We ask that you accept unlimited liability for losses the association may incur, should the computer malfunction." I was startled by these unreasonable demands put forward by the Japan Racing Association.

Kanjiro Okada, the Fujitsu President, saw it in a different light: "This is an excellent opportunity! Shouldn't we accept the unlimited liability condition? In any event, our very existence as a computer company means we are destined to bear unlimited responsibility. Let us confront this destiny, not try to avoid it. Let us rally the whole company and just see if we can't produce a machine that does not break down." His declaration excited everyone including myself.

Perhaps it is the nature of engineers to be inspired in this way—to rise to a challenge. This is what, in fact, happened. Because on this cue, a mood was created in which everyone strove to provide products and systems with extraordinary reliability. It was the beginning of Fujitsu's "High Reliability Campaign."

No matter how much confidence you have in your product, or how precisely it is made, machines are subject to failures—You cannot reduce this probability to zero. So what do you do? The Japan Racing Association's system utilized the FACOM 230-10, a small mainframe, operated with a tiered backup configuration. If you had one computer handling all the betting windows and that system were to go down, all the windows would have to be closed. Therefore, in our system, the windows were divided into groups and small computers, let's say for example, ten machines, were assigned to these groups. Then as a backup, five auxilliary computers were added, one for every two of the original group. With this arrangement there was no need to be apprehensive about a disturbance resulting from a total shutdown.

This tiered backup system was devised because we were acting on the fundamental premise that machines, being machines, breakdown. So successful was this type of system that eventually it was put into operation at racetracks throughout the country. The methods used were appropriate for the level of technology available at the time. Since then, we have organized numerous special projects to advance the reliability level of our systems, and on three occasions proposed ways of upgrading the original racetrack system. In the spring of 1982, our very large mainframe general purpose computer, the FACOM M-200 multi-duplex system (four CPU configuration) went into operation in the world's largest totalizator on-line network system.

Over the past decade, thanks to Fujitsu systems, there has been no trouble at the race tracks like the Toride incident mentioned above. Machines are never flawless but due to the carefully designed systems, there has not been even one chaotic incident due to a failure in one of the computers.

In a similar vein, from time to time there are reports in the newspapers of incidents occurring at bank teller windows. But here too, such troubles rarely arise at banks using Fujitsu computers. Should a failure or breakdown occur, it does not directly affect the teller's window. In other words, the systems have been designed so that a failure does not propagate itself throughout the entire system.

I think Japanese computer users are the most demanding in the world. If a problem arises and you do not immediately go to fix it or otherwise respond appropriately, they will not buy from you again. I think it fair to say that the performance of many Japanese products compares favorably with the level in other countries, because of being forged by the pressures and demands of our domestic market.

RELIABILITY BEGINS WITH DESIGN

I described above how, sparked by the Japan Central Horse Racing Association's "unlimited liability contract," the "High Reliability Campaign" became a company-wide drive. In 1966, under the chairmanship of Hanzo Omi, a Fujitsu Executive Director, a "Campaign Steering Committee" was inaugurated. About that time, "zero defects" (ZD) initiatives introduced from America were very popular. Our High Reliability Campaign, however, was not simply concerned with reducing "defects," which seems to me a rather passive approach. Our fundamental aim was to build an active drive to improve performance. That is, in all areas of the company, from research and manufacturing to sales and support functions, we expected each person to set goals for their individual work. These targets were independently established from the bottom up. In order to achieve them, we placed great emphasis on striving to stimulate creativity.

In 1982, I was invited to participate in a symposium in England sponsored by the *Financial Times* on "World Electronics." The speech I gave was entitled, "Is Japan the New Pacesetter?–Reliability and Creativity." It dealt with the "High Reliability Campaign." The following is the gist of my address on that occasion.

The first essential element in "reliability" is a high quality, finished product. To be precise, this means a low failure rate or few breakdowns. This in turn produces in the user a sense of the product's "reliability." A low failure rate is just as important to the manufacturer as it is to the user. This is because the manufacturer can then free human and material resources which might otherwise be required for repairs. And with fewer failures, in the event one does occur, it is then possible to provide immediate service.

I think Japanese televisions, tape recorders, and so on have achieved such a favorable reputation throughout the world because of their high level of reliability. It is taken for granted in Japan that televisions simply do not breakdown, or if they do, they are quickly and easily repaired.

If it is important for equipment such as televisions owned by private individuals to have a high degree of reliability, think how much more critical reliability is for important public systems. Take for instance Japan's Shinkansen bullet train system. The trains are controlled by computers. But since they began operation, there has not been even one accident involving the death or injury of a passenger. Or consider the telephone system: Telephone switching equipment uses electronics just as computers do, but it is a rare occurrence in Japan to fail to make a connection (other than, of course, when you get a busy signal) because of equipment failure.

Finally, consider the on-line services of the banking system: Deposits and withdrawals are managed with the help of on-line computers. If customers did not have access to their accounts due to a computer failure, there would be claims against the bank, and its trustworthiness would be called into question. Thus banks demand the utmost reliability in their computer systems.

We can see that the reliability requirements for public systems are very strict. Naturally, a very high degree of reliability is essential in the computers and electronic components at the core of these complex systems. However, since "reliability" is not something that can be measured in some precise, prescribed fashion, all the user can do is to trust the manufacturer.

The second element of "reliability" is the reliability level of the manufacturing process. In other words, this refers to not producing defective goods, and raising the ratio of usable product or yield. Improvement of the yield means, of course, lowering the manufacturing cost. But experience has shown that it also serves to increase the reliability of the finished product.

Quality control in Japan has in recent years become famous world wide. At Fujitsu we call the effort to make high quality products the "High Reliability Campaign." As can be seen in our quality control circles and related activities which are one element of this drive, each individual worker takes responsibility for his or her particular task and must strive to increase the reliability of their work.

In recent years the processes used in the electronics industry (in semiconductor manufacturing for instance) have made tremendous strides in miniaturization and integration. On this microscopic level, as the density—the number of transistors or other components—on a chip increases, unless there is a corresponding increase in reliability built into the process, you will not be able to produce a usable product. Even when the circuit design is correct, if the ratio of good product is small, you end up producing a mountain of defective devices. Semiconductor memory chips provide a good example. The scale of integration of mass produced chips has recently quadrupled, going from 256 kilobit to 1 megabit chips. If the yield of usable 256K chips is say fifty percent, and we were simply to integrate four 256K chips onto one 1M chip, the effective yield would be only 6.3 percent. Obviously, unless you have high reliability on your production line, you cannot make this kind of product or device.

If increasing the scale of integration is taken to be the mark of progress in electronics, then we will find the "pace-setter" wherever the manufacturing of increasingly large-scale integrated devices is conducted with the highest degree of reliability. In this sense, I believe we can say Japan is fully qualified to be a pace-setter.

The third aspect of reliability is related to design. The integration of semiconductors has increased rapidly from IC's (integrated circuits) to LSI's (large scale integration), and has moved into VLSI (very-large-scale integration). In the area of microprocessors, just a short time ago we had devices with a few thousand gates. Now, processors with from ten thousand to hundreds of thousands of gates are being sold. On this LSI level, a mistake in even one gate is unacceptable.

In the past, computers were designed, and a prototype produced, by trial and error. After a machine was up and running, mistakes in design were discovered. There were even instances of flaws in design being discovered after a system was delivered to the user. In such cases, it used to be possible to do some rewiring and replace a few printed circuit boards. When it comes to LSI's, however, repairs are more difficult. If there happens to be a defect in the design of an LSI, there is no other way to correct the problem than by replacing it with a newly designed LSI. Even if there is a mistake in only one gate out of tens of thousands, those tens of thousands of gates must be replaced. The cost involved is very high.

Of course there have been advances in the tools used for design. Unfortunately, despite the designer's use of such tools, other than actually producing the LSI chip and testing it, at present there is no other method to check for flaws in design. Since we must depend on this method, we have to demand the highest standards of "reliability" from our designers. Only those manufacturers with confidence in the "reliability" of their design will be able to go beyond the level of tens of thousands of gates and challenge the VLSI level with its hundreds of thousands of gates.

About a hundred and fifty meters above sea level, at the foot of Mt. Fuji, stands the Fujitsu Numazu Factory. From a vantage point near the factory Mt. Fuji looks especially beautiful. You can also gaze over the city of Numazu below. It is truly a place worthy of being called an industrial park. On the computer component assembly floor of the Numazu factory, there is an employee doing a remarkable job of using his "creativity" to enhance the "reliability" of our products. This example involves the process of attaching IC's to the main printed circuit boards. Each of the many individual pins protruding from the semiconductor package must be soldered to the main board. It is a delicate, painstaking process. If there is a mistake made with the soldering, the component will not work properly. Although IC's are very sensitive to heat, a thin, one or two millimeter strand of solder has to be applied.

Our Numazu employee thought there must be a way of soldering dozens of pins accurately at the same time. The scheme he devised was this: A sheet of paper with one or two millimeters solder-size holes punched where solder should be applied is prepared. Ring-shaped solder is then placed on the holes. When a soldering iron is applied from above, the paper burns and disappears and dozens of soldered connections are accomplished in an instant.

This soldering process used to require ninety people. Thanks to this employee's inventiveness, it can now be done by two people, and done more accurately. I presented him with an award in appreciation for this contribution. It is the cumulative effect of such individual creativity that has increased the reliability of Fujitsu computers. Thanks to these efforts, the failure rate of Fujitsu computers has been greatly reduced.

I was having dinner one time with the employee responsible for service and maintenance at Fujitsu Australia. He told me, "We don't have anything to do here because Fujitsu equipment never breaks down." "It has been my experience," I responded, "that no matter how precisely and carefully a machine is constructed, there is never a guarantee that it will not at some point fail. If you have no actual experience fixing a piece of equipment that is out of order, when the time suddenly arrives to do so, you won't know what to do. Therefore, it is necessary to intentionally cause a breakdown and see what you have to do. During the war, in the days when we really couldn't depend on machines, I'll tell you what we did. Like the fire department used to conduct regular fire drills, we would, for practice, purposefully put a piece of equipment out of repair and clock ourselves to see how long it took to repair it."

"A PEACH" OF A COMPUTER

About fifteen years ago there was a subsidiary of the trading company, C. Itoh, called C. Itoh Electronic Computing Service (currently known as Century Research Center). The company was involved in computer import sales and computing services. They used high speed computers from Control Data Corporation (CDC), the CDC-3600 and 3200 which were known at the time as the "best large scale high performance computers in the East." Control Data Corporation, founded in 1957, was a young company. But by that time, it had already established a unique position for itself as a manufacturer of very large and large scale computers, and as a provider of sophisticated scientific and technological computation services. Following the CDC-3600, in 1963 they announced the CDC-6600, a milestone in computer history, which is still in use around the globe today. Not only is CDC a superb company technologically, it is also a company imbued with a fighting spirit. In the face of constant hostility from IBM, they met the giant's strategy head on and even filed an antitrust action against them.

In any event, I had the honor of being a member of the board of directors of C. Itoh Electronic Computing Services and although I never requested that they use a FACOM computer, they must have felt some obligation to do so because in 1965, when they set up a branch office in Osaka, they installed a FACOM 230-25.

A short time after this, I ran into one of their executives and we had this exchange: "Mr. Kobayashi, the computer you sold us is a real peach." I replied, "Peach, what do you mean, it's a peach?" The executive responded, "You know, sometimes you buy a car, for example, and it turns out to be a lemon—You have one problem after another. A FACOM never breaks down. That's why I said it's a real peach." "Don't be absurd," I told him, "That's one of our standard models—They are all like that."

Underlying my friend's attitude was the assumption that a computer is something that has frequent breakdowns. C. Itoh Electronic Computing Services subsequently added a number of Fujitsu computers (At present their core machine is an American Cray Research super computer, the Cray-1. Along with this, they are using the FACOM M-190). From the user's point of view, machine failure is a terrible disruption. Put another way, there is no better way to please a customer than to eliminate breakdowns. The importance of this was brought home to us time and time again.

In a later chapter I will discuss the Amdahl Corporation in the United States in some detail. Here, I would just like to mention the 470-V. Fujitsu manufactures and exports the core sections of computers designed by Amdahl. The first computer produced this way, a 470 V/6, went to NASA, the American National Aeronautics and Space Agency. That broke the ice, and sales of the 470V series exploded. The first year, thirteen systems were sold. By the end of 1984, a total of more than a thousand of these computers had been shipped. Amdahl sales revenues went from 15 million dollars is 1975 to 190 million dollars two years later. Nine years later, in 1984, sales had multiplied almost 50 times to reach a figure of 780 million dollars. We were surprised, and I do not think the people at Amdahl anticipated such rapid growth.

It may well be that sales channels opened up as well as they did because of Dr. Amdahl's reputation and IBM compatibility. But I think it was more because we earned the trust of the people who are actually using our computers. In every single case, the machines went into full operation from 18 hours to two or three days after delivery. After installation there were very few breakdowns. To take an extreme example, because the 470V is plug compatible, if it were carried in on a Saturday morning, and all the plugs connected, on Monday morning the people arriving for work would notice that the machine had changed but there would have been no interruption of their work. Amdahl stressed this aspect of the system with the slogan: "Switch over now, we'll have your new computer up and running during your lunch break."

The 470 V/6 was sold to two life insurance companies during its first year on the market. One day a call came in from one of these insurance companies, "Are Fujitsu computers built to meet military specifications?" It seems they were curious as to why there were so few breakdowns. Although, of course I responded that they were our standard, not special military specifications, it was hard to get the caller to believe me. High technology in America has different specifications depending on whether a piece of equipment is for military or civilian use. The military has very stringent requirements. America, of course, has the technology to manufacture systems that do not break down, but the trade-off is a doubling or tripling of the cost. In Japan, the cost of products are the same whether they are delivered to the Defense Agency or to private industry.

Computers are fundamentally a conglomeration of LSI's, and for LSI's you have to have highly reliable manufacturing technology or you will not succeed.

I have already mentioned how a tiered backup system was used for the Japan Central Horse Racing Association's totalizator in their parimutuel betting system. The notion of strict checks so that accidents or mistaken calculations never come to the surface was fundamental to the thought of the late Toshio Ikeda, a computer genius and Fujitsu Board Director. Even as reliability increased as the basic elements of computers changed from transistors to IC's to LSI's, Ikeda stressed the necessity for having a perfect checking function in the CPU. "It's much better," he believed, "that a mistaken answer not be output," even if it increased the cost by 10 or 20 percent.

THE TWIN PILLARS: RELIABILITY AND CREATIVITY

Coverage of the "IBM Industrial Spying Incident" in the summer of 1982 gave a lot of play to the notion that although Japanese computer hardware is excellent, there is a weakness in the area of software. I would like to take issue with this idea. Only the naive or the non-specialists are of the opinion "Japanese software is weak." Other companies aside, I believe it is correct to say that Fujitsu software rather than being superior, is made to outperform IBM's. For example, Fujitsu was quick to provide financial support for Amdahl Corporation and was especially asked by Amdahl to manufacture the core components in the computers they are now selling. The system created can run the IBM operating system (OS) as is. An operating system, the basic system software, is a series of programs which allows the computer to operate at optimum efficiency.

Amdahl Corporation computers are being used in the most sophisticated environments including NASA, AT&T and its Bell Laboratories. Since they are completely compatible with IBM machines, the IBM OS can be utilized without modification.

On one occasion, a potential user approached us with this request. "We are considering purchasing an Amdahl computer but worried about the possibility of problems arising in our programs while running them with the IBM OS on your system. If we had no alternative in such a situation, we would really be in trouble. We would like to test the Amdahl running the Fujitsu OS instead of the IBM OS."

A group of them were invited to our company to test their software (user programs) on our system. In the process, it became evident that their software ran better on Fujitsu's OS than IBM's. Needless to say, they were greatly impressed. There is no better way to make a strong sales point for your system than to have excellent engineers come, conduct tests, and evaluate the performance. Because engineers make an objective appraisal, this kind of outside evaluation stimulates further sales. Because we realize that this becomes part of our international record, Fujitsu tries to be open as possible and makes every effort to invite guests from abroad to tour our factories and research facilities.

In any case, Fujitsu's OS was designed to be able to run IBM application software, although our operating system itself is not used on IBM machines. If Fujitsu does not have enough strength, we will have to resign ourselves to a role something like a subcontractor for IBM. If, however, we have the strength to exceed IBM, we will gradually eat away at IBM's market.

Another criticism often heard these days is that there is

no originality in Japanese technology or that it is lacking in creativity. This is not correct. From my perspective as an engineer, I have to say that these are criticisms of people who do not know what is actually happening. Consider for example optical transmission. One of the most advanced technologies of the 80's, it has given rise to fierce competition to develop and market new products based on this leading edge technology. Not many people know, however, that the first patent on the principles of optical transmission was obtained by a Japanese.

In 1936 a group lead by Hiroshi Seimiya at the Electrical Laboratory of the Communications Ministry obtained a patent on "a transmission medium which by interior reflection can send a light signal over long distances." I might add that Hiroshi Seimiya was my predecessor as President of Fujitsu.

At present, optical transmission is conducted by sending a beam of laser light through fine glass or polymer fibers. Our technology for manufacturing optical fibers has come under American patent attack, but I would ask you not to forget that the original idea for this new technology came from Japan.

Nippon Telegraph and Telephone (NTT) is now proceeding with its plan to construct a nationwide Information Network System (INS). A trunk line for the optical transmission systems network will extend from Hokkaido in the north to Kyushu in the south. The optical fiber cable is now being put into place, with completion planned for 1986.

Where creativity is concerned, I think for a manager or administrator (not the specialized scientist where the situation is a bit different), it has to arise from a close adherence to one's work. Then creativity manifests the way in which the reliability of that work can be increased and begins to be an effective tool. When creativity and reliability are in sync, outstanding performance becomes possible.

It is also a great mistake to think that Japanese computers are simply a copy of American computers. Professor Howard H. Aiken at Harvard built the Mark I relay style computer in 1944. At the same time, in spite of the disruptions of the Pacific War, Shinsuke Shiokawa of Fuji Electric Company built a relay digital calculator. Naturally, Shiokawa was not aware of the fact that the same thing was being done on the other side of the Pacific. The computer created in 1956, employing parametron elements, was also a totally original Japanese development.

In 1980, Fujitsu Laboratories announced the successful development of a completely new type of transistor, the High Electron Mobility Transistor (HEMT). A great variety of possible applications from computer memory and logic circuits to microwave transmission and optical transmission systems are being studied for this versatile device.

In 1982 Fujitsu began marketing Fortran 77, a high level programming language, in the United States. The critical response has been excellent. It makes program development easier; its high quality eliminates bugs; and it can be used without modification on IBM equipment. Research institutes in Europe and America evaluated it for us and gave it high marks. Thus, we became the first Japanese computer manufacturer to begin exporting software. Although it may become the source of additional trade friction, our Fortran 77 represents such an obvious example of quality, how can anyone say, "Japan is weak in software?"

Creativity is also manifested in the way organizations are structured. Fujitsu semiconductors are made in the best way possible to get the highest performance from our computers. To achieve higher computation speeds or greater integration, the LSI designers often work together with computer circuit engineers in a unified project team. Creativity working alone is frequently like riding a bicycle with the kickstand down—You peddle but the bike goes nowhere. It is when you have a target, like increasing reliability, that creativity really comes alive. I am fond of saying, "Hey, let's give it a try. I don't put my trust in something a book says, or something somebody else has done." What I mean is that even in the case of generally accepted facts, you should experiment yourself, gather and build up your own data. That is the source of creativity.

Kanjiro Okada used to say: "Copy? Our technology will never grow that way. If it's something from abroad, unless you really make it your own, you won't be able to do anything with it." In this company we call Fujitsu, time and again we see instances of employees badgering their bosses with, "Give it to me to do. Let me do it this way." And I think it no exaggeration to say that this has been the driving force behind Fujitsu's growth.

V

AMDAHL CORPORATION

Encounter with Dr. Amdahl while groping for a route to compatibility. Our good fortune to have cooperated formed the basis for today's success.

THE NECESSITY FOR COMPATIBILITY

As I indicated in the previous chapter, Fujitsu was able to become number one in Japan because of our dedication to the fundamental ideas of reliability and creativity. Our strategy, of course, was to take the path of IBM compatibility. For this, we were fortunate to be able to have joined forces with Amdahl. Since it is no exaggeration to say that our encounter with Amdahl determined the route that led to today's Fujitsu, I would like to discuss this in some detail.

When Fujitsu exhibited the FACOM 231 at the New York World's Fair in 1964, the idea of compatibility had not yet entered our plan. We learned, however, to our chagrin during that experience just how serious a handicap the lack of compatibility was. We discovered too that this was especially true when trying to export computers to a mature market.

Fujitsu's first venture into international business was

with the Philippines and Bulgaria. The Philippine business was related to World War II reparations. It was not much different from domestic sales, and compatibility was not an issue. In the case of Bulgaria, because it was part of the communist bloc, IBM had not made major inroads into the market. Consequently, we thought that we might well be able to market our computer in a region such as this.

Having achieved reasonable success in these two instances, we thought, why not America? We exhibited at the New York World's Fair but were simply not taken seriously. Fujitsu had not established technological ties with Univac, Honeywell, RCA, General Electric, or any of the American computer companies. Notice was taken of the independently developed Japanese computer but IBM's inner citadel failed to crumble; we did not make a single sale.

Shortly after this, however, we were approached by an American company, Automatic Science, Inc. (ASI) with an offer to market our computers in the United States. They had heard about our system at the New York World's Fair and were aware of our reputation in the other countries mentioned. Fujitsu gave ASI exclusive sales rights in a limited number of states. Although ASI spent a large sum of money on promotion, and seemed to be making every effort to sell the FACOM 230-25, not one was sold.

When our one-year contract expired, we were forced to terminate our agreement with them. Six months later, however, ASI brought suit against us. Their claims were a mixture of fact and fiction: "Sales were unsuccessful because of Fujitsu's uncooperative attitude, including their unilaterial termination of the contract. We therefore demand compensation for damages sustained because reasonably anticipated profits were not realized."

From our standpoint, it was a completely baseless, unfounded action, not to say a tremendous nuisance. As the defendent in the suit, we had no other recourse but to respond. The result was seemingly endless court proceedings stretching over a period of eight years. In 1980, Fujitsu won the suit, and the 100 million yen in legal fees and other expenses forced our opponent into bankruptcy.

In the meantime, we recognized that FACOM computers, despite the generally acknowledged reliability of the hardware, were not selling primarily because the software was not well suited to the user's requirements. Regardless of how much we could boast in Japan that our technology was second to none, unless we could, without modifications, run the same software created for IBM systems on our computers built around the same architecture, we would never be able to compete in the international market. In America, the most widely used system was IBM's. There was a large quantity of software for these systems that data processing people were very familiar with. Fujitsu's whole-hearted devotion and extremely reliable hardware were not enough: Compatability was essential.

With this in mind, we established Fujitsu California in 1968. An elite corps of our best engineers was selected and dispatched for "boot camp" in the United States. The objective was to accumulate technological expertise, put our technology to the test in America, and master the skills required to operate on an international scale. This was not only for Fujitsu; we thought it would, at the same time, come to serve the cause of other related industries. I should add that Fujitsu California experienced excellent growth and became what is today Fujitsu America, Inc.

During the first half of the 1960's, the Japanese markets were still only partially open to the international trading community. By the end of the 1960's, liberalization of trade had been stepped up and a schedule for the phasing out of trade restrictions put in place. We were about to enter a period of truly open markets and the Japanese government was busily readying the domestic economy for this development.

In 1964, IBM announced their 360 series which made full use of integrated circuits. The 360 series was a breakthrough which made possible a substantial reduction in both the size and cost of mainframe computers. It seemed the age of computers had now truly arrived.

In the fall of 1965, Fujitsu also began the development of an integrated circuit computer—the FACOM 230-60. Under the leadership of Toshio Ikeda, Manager of Computer Engineering, who was at that time still in good health, our company rose to the challenge of producing a top-of-the-line machine which would surpass the IBM 360 in computation speed, performance, and overall system specifications.

This 230-60 was completed in 1968 and, as I related in Chapter Three, the first one was installed at the Kyoto University Computer Center. The success of the 230-60, the computer Fujitsu is said to have "bet its future on," inspired confidence throughout the domestic computer industry because it was built with home-grown technology. Within Fujitsu, computer revenues moved ahead of the communications division revenues and were on the verge of overtaking the computer sales proceeds of our competitor, NEC.

Nevertheless, even if we were able to surpass our powerful domestic rivals, the situation in the international market was still the same: With computers that could not take advantage of software already widely used throughout the world, breaking the barrier into new markets would indeed be difficult. It was at this point that our encounter with Dr. Amdahl took place.

As I have indicated, Fujitsu had been considering the "compatible course" since well before the meeting with Amdahl. We were, so to speak, holding those cards for possible play. It was that meeting, however, which was finally decisive. We put our cards on the table and opted for the compatibility route.

ENCOUNTER WITH DR. AMDAHL

The IBM 360 series marked the dawn of a new era. The central figure and designer of the system was a high-level IBM engineer, Dr. Gene M. Amdahl. He was a man accorded prominence for his distinguished contributions at IBM. Prompted by a certain incident, however, he left the company. According to the information I have at hand, this is what seems to have happened. Around the beginning of 1969, Dr. Amdahl was the director of an IBM advanced computer research facility in Menlo Park, California. It was located in what has since come to be known as Silicon Valley. He was studying the market prospects for the next generation of high-end mainframes—the 370 series. The 370 series promised to be a new departure in computers for it was designed to use the newly developed "Medium Scale Integrated Circuits" (MSI) throughout.

Top management thought they should produce just one "top-of-the-line" model but the results of the research done by the group directed by Dr. Amdahl indicated otherwise. They determined that "a single high-end model will lead to red ink. Unless we build at least three models, including two smaller versions, we will not come up with a reasonable profit." Proposals to such an effect were made to senior management. Not only were they rejected, a few months later the research facility was closed down. With this, Dr. Amdahl's dream of selling the models he designed with the IBM label evaporated along with the research institution.

For one year after this, Dr. Amdahl was confronted with the choice: Should he continue to live within IBM or bolt the company to develop and produce himself the computer he wanted to build? It happened that Dr. Amdahl became director of a consulting company managed by his younger brother. IBM made its displeasure with this situation explicit, and this became the decisive factor in his leaving.

Word of Dr. Amdahl's troubles with IBM was passed along to me. The information was supplied to us by a person named Rodriguez of Litton Industries through Hanzo Omi, a Fujitsu director. Later, when Dr. Amdahl founded Amdahl Corporation, Mr. Rodriguez became one of the partners.

We had been seeking a means to international compatibility so we immediately decided to contact Dr. Amdahl. Toshio Ikeda, who had taken charge of our computer division, was dispatched to the U.S. in November of 1969. Ikeda was so highly regarded, he was even known in the United States as "Mr. Computer in Japan." He had his own unique conception of design represented, for instance, by the backup checking configuration built into the main processor which I have already mentioned. An extremely self-confident individual, he also had a streak of the romanticist. He was magnanimous, broad-minded. Honestly moved by other people's work, he would modestly offer his own evaluation.

His counterpart, Gene Amdahl, while still active in the industry, is already legendary. It is said that he will be remembered in history as a computer genius. An American of Norwegian ancestry, with bearing and countenance a bit on the stern side, he seems more like a pioneer out of the annals of the opening of the Western frontier than an engineer. He conveys a real sense of intensity.

One example of his genius, which does not begin to tell the whole story, is his design for the 360 series. He unified the series from top to bottom with a single architecture: A feat which destroyed commonly accepted ideas about computers at the time, and a leap which ordinary engineers could not begin to imagine.

Naoya Ukai, Fujitsu Engineering Manager, who worked with Gene Amdahl over a long period, has said he was astounded countless times. One episode involved the number of printed circuit boards mounted with LSI's required for the design of a new model. When an Amdahl Corporation project group of engineers proposed that twenty-three would be the optimum number, Dr. Amdhal countered, "Twenty-three is too many. Totally uncompetitive. For the performance you want, it should be done with eight." Ukai thought to himself that "eight" was just a bit of showmanship and that they could probably get it down to about fifteen. They had another go at it and lo and behold, optimal conditions were obtained with eight boards! Although Amdahl delegated the various details of projects to different groups, he had in his head a perfect, completed diagram of the whole. His nature is such that unless presented with the optimal solution, he will absolutely refuse to be convinced.

On another occasion, an Amdahl engineer responsible for computer circuitry approached Ukai with a problem. The division function of the main processor was coming up with strange remainders. The engineer thought there was some mistake in the circuit design. Discovering that it was

Dr. Amdahl who did the design, a group of ten engineers involved in the project went to the President's office and confronted him with the problem. For about five minutes, Dr. Amdahl sat in concentrated thought. Then he rose deliberately and quickly wrote a few formulas on the blackboard which revealed their mistake. Top-notch engineers stood in awe.

In any event, when Amdahl and Ikeda, the computer geniuses of America and Japan, first met, they had from the outset a congenial, one might even say, "kindred spirit" type of relationship. There was certainly a mutual feeling of "let's get this done." While it was for business that they met, it was also a real person-to-person encounter, and the beginning of Fujitsu and Amdahl Corporations' long and intense association.

THE NEED FOR JOINT DEVELOPMENT

Gene Amdahl resigned from IBM in August of 1970 and founded the Amdahl Corporation. It was during a period when the economy was stagnating and friends warned him, "Don't get into the business of mainframe systems; you'll never be able to raise the money necessary."

In general, mainframe general purpose computer users are very conservative when it comes to replacing existing equipment. If, however, it were not necessary to make a new investment in software, that is, the replacement system were compatible with software presently in use, and it also represented a higher cost-performance level, there was ample leeway for the introduction of replacement systems. In other words, these were the two necessary conditions for new computers to be widely accepted in the mainframe computer market.

In this regard, Amdahl Corporation computers were thought to have reasonable prospects for success. The biggest hurdle, as Dr. Amdahl's friends had pointed out, was financing. It was not easy to raise the huge sums required for development over an extended period. Depending on the speed of their development, it was estimated that from 33 to 44 million dollars in capital would be necessary. And despite Dr. Amdahl's reputation, venture capital was not eager to come forth with such huge sums based solely on his "confidence." The founders finally persuaded the Heiser Corporation, a venture capital interest, to make an initial investment of 2 million dollars. In about three months these funds were depleted and at one point, it appears that Amdahl was notified by the Bank of America that there was not a single dollar in their account. In addition to the unfavorable economic climate, Amdahl's plan to challenge IBM with a compatible machine had few supporters, and this naturally caused a considerable anxiety among the venture capital investors. RCA had already failed and start-up computer companies, such as MASCOR, had recently gone bankrupt.

We, on the other hand, had a very different perspective. Fujitsu saw tremendous potential in joining hands with Dr. Amdahl, who knew so well the strengths, weaknesses, and overall situation of IBM. We very much wanted his plan to succeed.

Having, through Ikeda, evaluated Dr. Amdahl's talents highly, we agreed to invest 5 million dollars with agreements for patent licensing, and joint development. Our position was best expressed by Hiroshi Seimiya, then Fujitsu's Executive Vice-President: "Since Fujitsu has little experience doing business abroad, in America or elsewhere, we absolutely must not interfere in the day-to-day management. Our relationship should be on the technical and financial level only."

In the following year, 1971, we sent twenty to thirty engineers to Fujitsu California Laboratories (FCL) and put together a mixed team of Japanese and Americans. It is often said that the Amdahl engineers were people Gene Amdahl drew along with him from IBM when he resigned. He has confirmed, however, that this was not the case. The engineers were gathered from companies such as MASCOR which had recently gone under. When the Amdahl Corporation was founded, I am told, the only personnel from IBM were two secretaries and one individual from accounting. Of course, it seems some of the engineers recruited had been at IBM and worked under Dr. Amdahl before moving to MASCOR and other companies.

By September of 1972, Amdahl had been in operation for two years, but the prospects for the release of their first system were still far from certain. Their financial difficulties continued and word came from the German company, Nixsdorf Computers, that they were interested in investing 6 million dollars in Amdahl. Because their participation would have significantly weakened Fujitsu's position as a major shareholder, we were constrained to make an additional investment equivalent to the Nixsdorf offer.

In the beginning, the predominantly young staff joined forces enthusiastically in the development effort. The strengths of both Amdahl and Fujitsu were combined in a manner that approached an ideal cooperative venture. Everyone involved in the United States tended to see the world through rose-colored glasses.

With the announcement that the first shipment of the 470-6 was scheduled for the following year, toward the beginning of 1973, Amdahl prepared to make a public offering in its final capital raising drive. These plans were thwarted first by the slumping stock market where the public offering twice fell through, and next by the jolting news that IBM was coming out with a new model totally unanticipated by industry observers.

Amdahl Corporation, with nowhere in the United States left to turn to for financial support, came to us with a request for assistance. Our response was this: "We would be happy to provide financial assistance, but that alone does not benefit us a great deal. We also want to be involved in production."

At first Dr. Amdahl thought that if Fujitsu would simply provide the funds, Amdahl could design and produce the computers. This was because he did not believe Fujitsu was capable of making highly reliable machines.

On our part, after observing their manufacturing process, we did not think they could produce a machine that would operate well. They purchased IC's, printed circuit boards, literally everything from outside vendors. Only assembly was performed by Amdahl. Since all our components were produced internally, we had gathered comprehensive data on the reliability of each part. This is because a computer consists of an extraordinary number of individual parts and if the accuracy of this part or that part is off by just a little, the overall reliability of the whole system suffers dramatically.

Another point that should be made is that from the outset we were not concerned with just copying IBM, but were considering how to create an operating system that would permit the use of software written to run on IBM machines (user programs). Amdahl was focused on only 360 series software. Consequently, when we proposed the use of a virtual memory or, somewhat later, the idea of multi-processors, the Amdahl side demurred. They thought it was enough to emulate the 360 architecture and the software for the 360 series.

IBM promptly stuck its first blow with the 370 series. The Operating System (OS) provided with the 370-168 (OS-MVS) employed a multiple-virtual memory and a part of the operating system was burned into the Read Only Memory (ROM) electronic circuitry. They also revealed plans for multi-processor systems.

The Fujitsu engineering group muttered to themselves, "Isn't it just as we expected?" With this the Amdahl side was finally convinced that Fujitsu should handle the software. They were, I suppose, developing a growing respect.

It was clear that with the introduction of the IBM 370 series, the Amdahl real memory 470-6 computer which was near completion would not have a very long product life. Plans for this machine had to be abandoned and development of a virtual memory compatible computer, the 470 V/6 begun immediately. These events forced Amdahl Corporation into its tightest spot to date.

Faced with a critical situation like this in Japan, a company would ordinarily contract its front line exposure and revise its strategy. Amdahl, in the so-called "American style" where "a little success is no success at all and only a resounding win is regarded as victory" seemed to simply continue in their previous manner, if anything, expanding their circle of operation as if courting risk.

Up to this point, Fujitsu had acted upon the principle of "non intervention in management." We knew very little about the day-to-day management and did not have a good understanding of their financial situation. Nevertheless, it had reached the stage where we felt we had to step in. Fujitsu had already invested about 4 billion yen and if that turned into a total lost, it would have shook our company to the foundation. Beyond that, we could not afford to abandon the beachhead we had worked so hard to establish in the United States.

Normally, it would have been appropriate for major share-holders, including Fujitsu and Heiser Inc., to improve their channels of communication regarding the management of Amdahl Corporation. But Dr. Amdahl, while he is an extraordinary engineer, was no genius when it came to management, and he disliked others intervening. It seemed he was not satisfied unless he did everything himself.

Even Seimiya, the Fujitsu Executive Vice President who had personally been opposed to Fujitsu's involvement in management, reversed himself and ordered "direct involve-ment in managerial decisions." A check revealed that although production goals for the first computer had not yet been established, there were already 760 people on the payroll. Notice was given that it was necessary to reduce that number by about 300 and that Dr. Amdahl should take managerial responsibility by relinquishing his position as President and assuming the position of Chairman.

During these negotiations, there occurred an incident—the "signed oath incident"—which I am sure that everyone involved at Fujitsu would very much like to forget. Since word had spread that about half the employees at Amdahl would have to be fired, various rumors hit the California Amdahl office: "There is a plot to provoke a financial crisis...A Fujitsu takeover bid was coming." All the Amdahl engineers—260 of them—signed an oath which Dr. Amdahl then took to Japan. They had all pledged: "If Fujitsu so much as lays a finger on the management of Amdahl, each and every one of us is prepared to resign."

A very awkward oppressive atmosphere surrounded Dr.

Amdahl and Executive Vice President Seimiya as they sat down to their meeting. Seimiya resolutely broke the silence, "I am afraid you are no longer President of the company. From now on we will be participating in the management of Amdahl Corporation."

Dr. Amdahl replied, "What do you mean kicking me, the founder of the company, upstairs to be Chairman! I will resign. This cannot be permitted. All the employees are against it."

Thereupon followed a desperate attempt to convince the red-faced, angry Dr. Amdahl to accede to our demands. Knowing as he did, that if Fujitsu were to withdraw, it would mean certain bankruptcy, there was not much more he could say. During this period, Amdahl Corporation had twice been within three hours of insolvency, had a timely check not been deposited. It was not unusual for employee paychecks to be distributed late.

Fujitsu employees working at Amdahl appear to have been told, "The order to leave may come at any time. So do your work this in mind." They spent their days trying to figure out how to best minimize the damage.

In the end, fortunately, an agreement was reached. Approximately one third of the work force, or 250 Amdahl employees were let go, and a new President, Eugene White, a consultant who had been with General Electric, was appointed. Under the firm managerial hand of Mr. White, Amdahl Corporation recovered marvelously. Even so, it would be unfair to deny the achievements of Dr. Amdahl. As a computer engineer, there was nobody better, and without him the success of today's Amdahl Corporation would not have been possible. It was simply the case that a genius at design does not necessarily have the same talent for management.

I am sure those were humiliating days for Dr. Amdahl, but this sequence of incidents also left sad memories among us at Fujitsu. The convulsive few months took its toll on Ikeda who had overall responsibility for the project. He traveled back and forth between Japan and the United States numerous times and had to face stomach-wrenching negotiation after negotiation.

Originally, as the person in charge of overseas operations, I should have been the one doing this exceedingly tough job. But I was still in the hospital recovering from the third operation on my stomach. I recall Ikeda saying to me when he visited the hospital, "I'll have no problem handling the negotiations; so, you please just rest and recuperate." Not long after this, in November of 1974 on his way to meet the President of Consolidated Computers Inc. of Canada (CCI) at Haneda Airport in Tokyo, Ikeda suffered a fatal stroke. He was only 51 years old. Shouldering my responsibilities as well as his own, as he rushed back and forth over the ocean, Ikeda's death can truly be said to have been a heroic one in the "vanguard of the battle." I still feel pangs of regret and sorrow. Not only did he die right before the 470 V/6 was shipped from our Kawasaki factory to Amdahl, but the Fujitsu M-190, which Ikeda had also overseen throughout its development, was announced just one week later. I wish he could have seen the birth of these computers during his life.

The Amdahl 470 V/6, a product of Japanese-American cooperation, built at the Fujitsu-Kawasaki factory and finished by Amdahl Corporation represented a new departure in the computer field. The first system was delivered to the American National Aeronautics and Space Agency (NASA) in June of 1975. IBM must have been surprised to see its performance! Its sister computer, the FACOM

M-190 was the machine that beat IBM in Australia, as I have related in the opening chapter.

The Amdahl computer was at first mainly manufactured by Fujitsu, then assembled into a system, and given final testing at Amdahl. As it was introduced by various companies, its reputation grew. It became a very popular model. Although it is at the high-end of mainframe computer systems, more than a thousand have been sold. I do not know of any other American venture business that has been so successful.

The time of Dr. Amdahl's troubles was also a period for major changes in Fujitsu's direction. It is no exaggeration to say that the experience of Amdahl and Fujitsu helping each other and overcoming so many difficulties, has since forged an inseparable bond between the two companies.

VI

COMPATIBILITY

Due to the development of IBM compatible FACOM systems we experience substantial growth in the international arena. Our advances in the United States, West Germany and Spain.

TEAMING UP TO OPPOSE IBM

After the completion of the FACOM 230-60 described in the previous chapter, we then had to consider how to achieve compatibility with our next series of mainframes. This series, known as the M series, was to be developed in cooperation with Hitachi with financial assistance from the government. It was this M series that ultimately defeated IBM in Australia.

About this time the Japanese government was ready to take steps to liberalize foreign investment regulations. In July, 1967, the Foreign Investment Commission issued its report which directed that:

1. Restrictions should be phased out in many areas by the end of 1971.

2. Concentrating on businesses with a foreign capital participation ratio of up to 50%, liberalization should proceed immediately (first group). Efforts should also be made to increase the number of 100% foreign capital enterprises (second group).

Based on this report, in July of 1967 the first phase of the liberalization was put into effect. The measures focused on 50 industrial categories (33 in the first group, and 17 in the second). Following this, in March of 1969, the second phase saw the liberalization expanded to include 154 additional industrial categories, and in September 1970, the third stage brought the inclusion of the automobile industry. After August, 1971, the fourth phase saw a change from "Restrictions in Principle, some exceptions free" to "Free in Principle, some exceptions restricted"—a negative list method.

Regarding the computer industry, however, the manufacturers in competition with IBM still faced a wide gap in technological development and international marketing strength. Because of the strategic importance of computers the industry was excluded from the liberalization up to the fourth phase. Even after this, however, the government exerted every effort to protect and nurture domestic computer manufacturers.

Along with the "Nixon Shock" in the summer of 1971 came increased demands from abroad for the opening up of Japan's domestic market. To respond to this, in the fall of 1971, under the administrative guidance of MITI, the six principal domestic computer companies were encouraged to form groups for mutual assistance with future development. Fujitsu was paired with Hitachi, NEC with Toshiba, and Mitsubishi with Oki. Each of these three groups began cooperative efforts to build systems to compete with IBM's 370 series. They were assisted by a subsidy program established by MITI in accordance with a five-year plan beginning in 1972 for the development of computers and peripheral devices.

As a result, during 1976 the Fujitsu-Hitachi M series,

the NEC-Toshiba ACOS series, and the Mitsubishi-Oki COSMO series were released one after another.

I believe Fujitsu was paired with Hitachi because of Hitachi's connection with RCA. The RCA Hitachi development of IBM compatible systems accorded with Fujitsu's own compatibility strategy. It is not generally known that when we heard Dr. Amdahl was going to leave IBM to form his own company, we approached Hitachi with the suggestion they join us in establishing a relationship with Amdahl. Thinking it was an excellent opportunity because of Amdahl Corporation's LSI technology, we established a connection with them, but Hitachi, for some reason declined, thus ending further discussions.

At the time, domestic computer manufacturers were squared off in severe competition and despite the groupings for cooperation, a rival was still a rival. The mass media jeeringly described the situation as "shaking hands with one hand while thrashing the partner with the other." This rather exaggerates the situation but it was in fact a strained "collaboration." During the feudal period in Japan, when there were constant wars and shifting alliances, the wives of the daimyos, or feudal lords, were often betrothed for strategic purposes. I do not think our collaboration with Hitachi was a "marriage for love" but like the daimyo's wives in a crisis, I believe they would fulfill their role. It is a good example of what I like to call "cooperation and competition."

Regarding the merits and demerits of MITI's computer development policy, I would like to make the following hopefully constructive comment. The MITI bureau directors and managers never remain at one post for as long as three years; they move up and change positions frequently. In our business, as I have indicated, we work in project teams. Consequently, over say a three-year period, we are not constantly moving from one position to another. Because of the difficulties this presents in maintaining close government-industry communication, only a fundamentally independent approach to developmental strategies is possible.

Looking back over recent history, one notes that MITI's original policy for helping the Japanese computer industry catch up with the advanced countries was to encourage the introduction of foreign technology. Fujitsu, which had opted to pursue an independent path, was called to task. Directors were summoned and told in no uncertain terms: "Fujitsu has chosen not to enter into technology licensing agreements with companies abroad. Very well, but do not expect us to bail you out."

Nevertheless, as liberalization of trade and investment policies proceeded apace, there was an abrupt change. All of a sudden pressure was on to develop 100% Japanese products. For a time MITI indicated that joint research with foreign companies was anathema, but recently they have become strong supporters of this kind of cooperative research. The frequent shifts and transformations of policy breed a kind of cynicism. Changes in government policy cause us difficulties but to cope by pointing the finger of blame at the government does not help because, of course, ultimately the industry itself has to resolve the problems. This is why industry must have independence. It may well be that firm decision making in this area is what distinguishes leaders in Japanese business management. It is certainly much easier to follow along doing just what the government advises but I do not think this can really be called good management.

COOPERATIVE DEVELOPMENT PROJECTS

The grouping of Fujitsu and Hitachi was of course accomplished due to the administrative guidance of MITI. At the same time, the fact that my predecessor, President Seimiya and Hitachi Executive Vice President Kubo were classmates and drinking companions also was a factor. That discussions moved along so smoothly, and the cooperation of both companies yielded such fine results, can be attributed to their close friendship.

For example, a committee of specialists was formed which worked on joint development projects and in operations a sales organization called FACOM-HITAC Limited (FHL) was established to handle sales to government agencies. It continues to do so today. Another example is the founding of Nippon Peripherals Ltd (NPL), a cooperative venture designed to help defray the tremendous expense of developing peripheral devices. NPL has been very profitable due to its successful development of high capacity magnetic disks and memory devices which automatically exchange magnetic cartridges. It has grown into an excellent company, expanded beyond the domestic market, and is now exporting in substantial volume to the United States and Europe.

Both companies were pleased with this aspect of the collaboration policy. I think there were definite benefits obtained from having engineers and technical people from different companies working side by side. Coming from different environments and holding different views, they experienced a cross fertilization of ideas that gave rise to new concepts and approaches to problems. Because Japanese companies have a life-time employment system, once an employee joins a corporation, his chances of ever getting an inside view of another company are practically nil. In Hitachi, because they are involved in a wide range of enterprises from heavy electrical equipment to semiconductors, employees have greater opportunity than we to move to different divisions and be stimulated by a new perspective. They do not ordinarily, however, have an opportunity to see how things work outside the Hitachi Group.

It can be said that cooperative development was a great stimulant: We showed each other our factories, exchanged opinions and, on occasion, fell into disagreement. Hitachi's way of thinking contributed greatly to Fujitsu's management techniques. I think it can probably be said Hitachi experienced a similar enrichment.

Once, when cooperative development projects were in full swing, I had the ill luck to be harshly upbraided by an American entrepreneur: It's crazy to publicly announce the aims of your research just because you want government subsidies. You get a little money, but what good does it do? Research and development plans are supposed to be the biggest industrial secrets a company has. To not only make them public but to actually work together with a rival company to accomplish your goals just does not make any sense." And to top it off, he then proposed, "Are you interested in working with us?"

Because he added those last words, I am not sure where he really stood, but looking at the success in Japan today, I think we can see that the Japanese approach in this instance was essentially correct. (It is doubtful, I might add, had we accepted this American's proposal at the time, whether things would have gone so well!)

TOWARD IBM COMPATIBILITY

Initially, there was opposition within Fujitsu toward the plans for cooperative development with Hitachi. From a business standpoint, resistance was centered around the idea that Fujitsu had set out to become the top computer manufacturer in Japan with its independently developed FACOM technology. However, the opening of the domestic computer market to competition from abroad was rapidly approaching. An IBM compatible strategy was essential. It would both enable us to defend the domestic market from outside forces, and, with our computers able to run IBM software, allow us to develop an international marketing plan.

Quite frankly, I myself had serious misgivings about whether we should publicly admit to being in the business of producing machines that could use the IBM operating system without any modifications. With these reservations in mind, Takuma Yamamoto and I negotiated directly with IBM Japan. IBM, we were told, would not make any information available. We then proceeded to develop our own Fujitsu OS so that IBM application software our customers possessed could be used when combined with an interface we designed.

At Fujitsu technologically we had absolutely no anxiety about being able to produce an IBM compatible machine. The component technology, computer architecture, software and so on represented no serious obstacles. On the question surrounding how users would evaluate our software—whether it would be considered to be fully compatible—there was some concern. As we shall see, however, these were needless worries.

While there may have been no problems on the technical side, the unknown element was simply how the compatibility strategy would work from a business point of view. It confronted IBM head on and compatible meant you were also opening up the gate to your own fortress. There was always the danger of being attacked. It was safer to continue behind those walls; but that eliminated real opportunity. It was unclear just how IBM would sally forth.

Dr. Amdahl had an excellent understanding of IBM's business nature. This was the advantage to be gained by investing in his company. I think it can be said that Fujitsu's compatibility route reached fruition—flowered and bore fruit—thanks to our relationship with Dr. Amdahl.

Success was secured by a number of other factors, as well as a certain amount of good luck. The first of these was that when Fujitsu and Amdahl Corporation began cooperative development, Fujitsu's autonomously developed technology—both hardware and software—had attained a level on a par with world standards. Had Fujitsu's technology not been up to that level, even with Dr. Amdahl, we would probably not have achieved anything like the success we have today.

The second major factor was Control Data Corporation's suit against IBM for anti-trust violations. The settlement reached in 1973 was in essence a total defeat for IBM and they loosened up considerably. Had Fujitsu been in IBM's position, and we saw another company producing low-cost, high-performance computers very similar (compatible) to our own, which were gradually taking away our market share, we would not have taken it lightly. From the beginning, I am sure we would have found this "compatibility" strategy unacceptable. That a plug-compatible company like Amdahl achieved such success, while it does reflect the particular circumstances IBM found itself in at the time, is another clear indication of, shall I say, the broadmindedness, or tolerance, or depth of the country called America. In any event, I feel there was a streak of good luck, a combination of fortunate circumstances behind our success.

I should mention that although both are compatible, Amdahl computers are completely compatible, while the FACOM M-series machines are not. This means that M series users who take full advantage of the FACOM OS cannot simple switch to an IBM machine: The software compatibility works only one way.

AT&T (American Telephone and Telegraph) is today using dozens of Amdahl computers. When Bell Laboratories was about to switch from IBM to Amdahl machines, their scientists were concerned about the possiblilities of major problems arising should restrictions be placed on IBM's operating system. They visited our Kawasaki Factory and ran their own programs on FACOM computers utilizing Fujitsu's own OS, testing for compatibility and performance. Needless to say, they were fully satisfied with the results. They made a special point of receiving assurances that we would "supply them with the FACOM OS if they faced a situation in which it was no longer possible to use the IBM OS on Amdahl computers."

After Amdahl Corporation succeeded, many voices could be heard asking the question "Why didn't American business come to the aid of Amdahl?" It seems it was a question raised even on Capitol Hill. The fault-finders had a field day: No one, not the venture capitalists, or the securities companies or others in the computer industry invested in Amdahl. The only one to come forth with money was a Japanese company. As a result, Japanese business has made a name for itself. Something must have gone wrong...

CUSTOMER TO CUSTOMER PROMOTION

Along with progress on the compatibility course and the strengthening of our technology development, came steady improvement in Fujitsu's position in the world-wide computer market. Very large scale and large scale mainframe computers are being built to the purchaser's specifications and exported to the United States through Amdahl Corporation. On-line financial systems are marketed directly by Fujitsu Systems of America. Fujitsu America, Inc. is developing, manufacturing and selling communications and data processing equipment. Semi-conductors and electronic components are handled by Fujitsu Microelectronics Inc. These are our four principle channels in the American market.

In Germany, technological ties were reestablished in 1979 with Siemens AG, the electrical manufacturing conglomerate, and mainframe computers are being exported there on an OEM basis. Siemens is in a sense a Fujitsu grandparent. Fuji Electric was born out of prewar cooperation between Furukawa Electric and Siemens. Fujitsu came into being in 1935 when the communications equipment division was separated from Fuji Electric and set up as an independent company. When Fujitsu was established in June of that year I moved to the new company and remember struggling with my German in technical discussions with German engineers. At the time it was everyone's desire to go to Siemens in Germany for study. Forty years later, the tables turned, I traveled to Germany on a sales mission. It gave me a real sense of how times have changed. The grandchild, I guess we could say, has now come of age.

Although we had a very close relationship with Siemens over the years, until the 1979 agreement there had been no technical arrangements in the area of computers at all. It probably has nothing to do with the fact that Fujitsu had once been on the receiving end of technological assistance, but Siemens had introduced technology from RCA and was producing a machine similar to IBM's. At first they appeared to harbor some doubts regarding Fujitsu's M series. Their reservations revolved around the question "We wonder how well it will work considering it is independently developed technology."

In January of 1975 I visited the Siemens' headquarters in Munich and met with Professor Gumin who was in charge of their computer business. When I heard that their computer division was troubled by losses, I suggested the following: "The problem is you are not doing anything with mainframes. The competition in the mini and smaller scale systems is so intense it is difficult to turn a profit. We are producing mainframes—our M series—and showing a good profit. Are you interested in giving it a try?" I then invited him to come to Japan to at least take a look at what we were doing. Professor Gumin, a rather proud individual, evidently had serious reservations regarding our M series but finally one of his subordinates, Mr. Ohmann, arrived in Japan to conduct an evaluation. He was greatly impressed with the results of his tests, and appears to have reported as much to top management upon his return home.

Soon after this Mr. Plettner became the Siemens' President and Mr. Peisle took over the responsibility for their computer business. Very quickly a close relationship was established, agreements for cooperation right across the board were reached, and Fujitsu began OEM exports. The models shipped were high end mainframes based on the FACOM M-180II, and M-200 which would supplement and complete the Siemens product line.

The first sales of Japanese mainframes in the European Economic Community, so long completely dominated by IBM, marked a major event in the history of the computer business. Plans for the first year called for the sale of only three systems. The expression "only three" was perhaps overly optimistic: Even with the support of Siemens, I do not think we could have reasonably anticipated a greater number of sales. Unexpectedly, however, powerful reinforcements appeared.

Siemens intended the first machine to go to the computer center of DATEV, a professional accounting firm with over 20,000 employees. DATEV, unfortunately, was not so easily persuaded. They were a long-time IBM customer and had leased a large number of IBM machines. No matter how many Siemens labels were pasted on the equipment, their response was, "This Fujitsu product never seen in Europe before is just too risky, we cannot use it."

The reinforcements I mentioned arrived in the person of Mr. Takeshi Iizuka, President of TKC, Inc., Japan's largest accounting firm and provider of computer services for regional governing bodies. TKC was a major Fujitsu customer. They had for a long time graciously honored us with their business. Mr. Iizuka (currently Chairman of TKC) was on very good terms with Mr. Sebiger the DATEV chairman in Nuremburg. He was kind enough to enthusiastically recommend FACOM to DATEV stressing the exceptional reliability of Fujitsu computers. Thanks to his wholehearted endeavor, Mr. Sebiger decided to replace one of the IBM backup computers with a Siemens model. Thus our first machine was installed. Before long, as it became evident that the Siemens computer not only experienced no failures but actually performed better than the main IBM machines, the IBM computers were steadily replaced by the

Siemens line. Finally, it reached the point where more than half the IBM computers were driven out. I sent a letter of thanks to Mr. Iizuka expressing my gratitude for his help.

Sometime later when I was in Nuremburg, a DATEV executive said to me "Even before your machine was installed, we started to see results." Asked what he meant, he replied "As soon as we said we were bringing in a Fujitsu computer, IBM's attitude changed abruptly. Before that, even if we had an order in, they wouldn't tell us when it was going to be installed or supply us with the information we requested. Now it's, 'You'll be the first to receive our new model.' All of a sudden, service has improved dramatically."

IBM today is not like it was: Service appears to have improved. Then, however, because it was an IBM monopoly market, I suppose they sat back with too much complacency. There is nothing like competition to benefit the customer.

In Europe, with promotion taking the form of a computer advertising itself through its reliability and performance, sales continued at a surprising pace. By the end of 1983 OEM shipments through Siemens exceeded 150 units.

I believe Mr. Iizuka, the TKC President, was willing to so convincingly argue our case because he truly valued the performance of the Fujitsu computers working for his company. In the final analysis it was our customers who opened up the European market for us, a market hitherto long dominated by IBM.

In this manner, both the excellence of Fujitsu technology employed in the Amdahl systems and the excellence of Fujitsu finished products such as the M series mainframes sold in Europe through our OEM business with Siemens came to be widely recognized throughout the world.

This was the situation when early in 1981 the Japanese

and British governments approached us to sound out the possibility of obtaining our cooperation in a plan to rebuild International Computers Limited. ICL, England's largest domestic computer manufacturer, was suffering from a serious decline in their business. As the only British computer manufacturer, they were putting up a valiant struggle but caught up in what has been called the "English disease" and faced with might of IBM's monopolistic market control, they were being forced into retreat. We immediately began a study to see what could be arranged between ICL and Fujitsu. In December of that year, technological and sales cooperation agreements were signed centered around the joint development of mainframe computers and the supply of semi-conductors.

At the June 1982 World Electronics Seminar sponsored by the *Financial Times* I delivered a lecture which examined some of the reasons behind the success of the Japanese computer industry. An ICL employee at the seminar asked what ICL could do to achieve the success of a company like Fujitsu. Since I have always thought that a spirit of challenge, a feeling of "you don't know until you try" is the most important element in a hi-tech industry, I replied, "You can't wait for directions from senior management. You have to develop a sense of will and creativity in your middle management and among ordinary employees so that you get together and get things done." My response brought unexpected approval from my audience and served to increase my confidence in the correctness of our approach to management.

We have found, by the way, that cooperation with ICL has been going smoothly not just at the top but in mid-level relationships as well. ICL products manufactured with this cooperation have already appeared on the market.

CULTIVATING AN INFORMATION
INDUSTRY IN SPAIN

The phenomenon of customers promoting our system to other customers or a "computer advertising itself" was not limited to Germany. We have seen it happen all over the world. Spain is another good example.

Fujitsu's first relationship with Spain was established over ten years ago. It began when the director of Spain's Foreign Investment Bureau visited Japan in April of 1972 during the Goya Exhibition in Tokyo. In order to develop Spain's data processing industry Fujitsu agreed to help with their domestic production of computer terminal equipment and mini-computers. The following year, 1973, the Chairman of Spain's Institute of National Industry (INI) met with us in Japan and definite plans were drawn up. In March 1973, with joint investments from INI, the Spanish National Telephone Corporation (CTNE) and Fujitsu, a national computer company SECOINSA (Spain Communication and Data Processing) was born. With absolutely no data processing industrial base to build on, introducing new technology and providing technical assistance was not an easy task. First of all, it required tremendous capital expenditures. Putting our calculators to work, we figured out that if they purchased Fujitsu computers and we applied the payments toward the costs of technical assistance, we could probably just about break even.

As a result of our negotiations with CTNE, it was decided in September 1974 that CTNE would terminate the leases on five IBM 370's it had been leasing, and install the FACOM M-190, Fujitsu's largest computer at the time. Naturally IBM responded with a fierce counter offensive.

They immediately offered an extremely low cost purchase option on the leased machines and managed to get CTNE to purchase all the IBM computers. We were worried that they would put plans to use the M-190 on an indefinite hold. An agreement is an agreement, however, and in December of 1976, the purchase contract for the first two units was signed. CTNE at that point still had not decided how the system would be utilized. A proposal to put it to use in a backup service that CTNE operated for the banking association was considered but this plan was ultimately rejected. Finally, just before the machine was to be shipped, delivery was changed from their information processing center to the EDP department responsible for internal processing operations. Possibly due to their anxiety over using a new system for the first time, the EDP department came up with very stringent conditions to be met regarding compatibility with the three IBM machines already in use and performance levels expected.

We simply urged them to give it a try and see for themselves. When the system was finally installed a year later, in December 1977, they conducted a thirty day test run. There were no problems with compatibility. In terms of performance comparisons it was two to three times better than the machines they had been using. Needless to say, their anxieties vanished into thin air.

One of the individuals in charge, in a passionate manner characteristic of the Iberian people, praised our efforts, with words I was delighted to hear. "It's wonderful; we have never before had such responsive service. You see things from the user's standpoint and respond accordingly." When we met with the Director General and executive staff they expressed their satisfaction and even wanted to "Thank Fujitsu for helping to improve the service of other companies."

The IBM machines they had gone to all the trouble to purchase were, irreverently, one after another, disconnected and moved to provincial centers. In their place the second and third systems remaining in our contract were installed. Over the next sixteen months CTNE purchased an additional five M Series computers for use in different regions of the country.

While this was happening, the first national computer company in Spain, SECOINSA established in 1975, was slowly but steadily making progress. Operation began in a temporary factory in Malaga in May, 1977. They advanced from the production of modems (devices for connecting computers and telephone lines) to the production of the FACOM VIII office computer.

By April, 1979, when basic manufacturing techniques and quality assurance systems had been mastered, the new main factory was ready. They began to initiate their own research and development activities and toward the end of 1980 had not only started production of a new model minicomputer—the V-830—but had also developed their own switching device for a packet switching network. SECOINSA's marketing strength increased to the point where they were able to obtain the order for terminals for Iberian Airlines' seat reservation system.

Looking at the growth pattern of SECOINSA we can see that it takes a minimum of ten years for a computer manufacturing business to really take shape when the industry is built from the foundation up.

I would like to mention that CTNE's high evaluation of Fujitsu's products is reflected by the 1982 Madrid Telephone Directory which had gracing its cover a photograph of the FACOM M-190.

VII

RESEARCH AND DEVELOPMENT

The importance of creating an appropriate environment for innovative research. Our "intra-company venture business" approach—make money available but do not interfere—proves effective.

FROM JEF TO OASYS

Being able to use computers in Japanese was a long-cherished dream of manufacturers and users alike. Without Japanese language capability the prospects for computer growth in Japan looked dim. Since computers had been developed in the English speaking world, for a long time the prevailing presumption was that only English could be used. In February 1972, Fujitsu held a dedication ceremony for the International Social Science Research Institute which had just been completed. We invited Professor Eiichi Goto to deliver an address. Professor Goto, the inventor of the parametron, is a member of Faculty of Science at Tokyo University and the foremost authority on computers in Japan.

His logical, cogent argument that day highlighted the necessity for bringing Japanese language and computers together. "Written communication between software programmers is an extremely important factor in the efficient production of Japanese software. It is critical that ideas be transmitted quickly and accurately. With their poor English, Japanese, who are unable to converse in any language but their own, will never be able to catch up with America in computers if only English can be used. To overcome this difficulty, we have to develop computers able to output text in Japanese in the easy to read *Kanji* and *Kana* orthography. Because *Kana/Kanji* text—with its high information density—lends itself well to easy scanning, it can be read faster than Americans read English. If this were done, software development would advance rapidly."

There is no question we were dissatisfied with computers which could only handle English alpha-numerics and occasionally *Katakana*. We were also disturbed to be falling behind in software development. Listening to Professor Goto, we found ourselves in complete agreement. I do not know whether he really pulled the wool from our eyes, or merely inspired us with new confidence. In any event, he had clearly indicated the way we should proceed.

The Japanese language has two distinct syllablaries, *Katakana* and *Hiragana*, each with fifty-one characters which correspond to the phonetic alphabets in other languages. In addition, thousands of characters introduced from China centuries ago and known as *Kanji* are used to write the modern Japanese language. The language is normally written with a combination of *Kana* and *Kanji* giving Japanese one of the most complex orthographies in the world. Getting a computer to handle the full range of characters in Japanese presented formidable obstacles.

Nevertheless, stimulated by Professor Goto's talk, I took every opportunity after that to stress over and over again to our engineers the necessity for *Kana/Kanji* processing on our computers. Several months later I received a report indicating that progress had been made toward this goal. Subsequently, development proceeded at a feverish pitch and before long was consumated in a form known as JEF.

JEF stands for "Japanese processing Extended Feature." This development added the new capability of handling Japanese information in *Kana/Kanji* mode to the previous alphanumeric and *Katakana* input/output functions. The software was not just for Japanese; it added this function to our original software which is why it was called an "Extended Feature."

There were a number of problems that had to be dealt with in the development of JEF. Among them, the most difficult was keeping the cost down. We wanted to keep to within a 20% increase when compared with previous systems. This had to be done because if the cost were too high, regardless of the additional convenience of being able to process data in Japanese, users might not be so willing to switch to the expanded feature system.

What made it possible for us to keep the cost within this margin was the rapid advancement in semi-conductor technology. Large capacity IC memory chips, LSI's and microprocessors were introduced; production methods improved; and semi-conductor devices became available at a fraction of their previous cost. The elimination of unnecessary functions in our software also helped us to achieve our goal.

On the hardware side, special input devices were developed to add the *Hiragana* and *Kanji* function to *Katakana* and alphanumeric processing. A laser beam line printer was added to our product line, and it became possible to output text in standard (*Hiragana-Kanji*) Japanese form.

When JEF was announced in April 1979, needless to say, it received a tremendous response and was hailed as "ushering in a new age of computers for Japanese people." Thirty years after Fujitsu had brought forth its first computer, the Japanese language could now be used in a data processing environment. I expressed my deepest gratitude to the people who had labored long and hard to make it possible.

I have already described how when Fujitsu came out with the M-Series, due to its IBM capability, we began to cut into IBM's market share and attract existing IBM users. There were, at the time, those who rebuked us saying, "Aren't you just following in IBM's wake?" With JEF, however, we had produced something IBM did not have; something much better than IBM had to offer.

The "Japanese Processing Extended Feature" (JEF) can best be thought of as laying the foundation for the period of office automation (OA) we are in the midst of today. After our development of "Japanese language data processing," the next challenge was "Japanese language text processing." This meant devising a computer system capable of composing, revising and storing reports, manuals and other documentation in Japanese. One of the hardware devices developed for this task was the Japanese Language Word Processor.

A word processor is an electronic typewriter which enables the user to store composed documents in memory and recall them to make additions, deletions and other changes. The text is displayed on a CRT while it is being entered from a keyboard. Various editing functions can be carried out by striking a few keys. Once a document or graphic composition has been stored in memory, it can be called up any number of times for reference, revision or other purposes.

In 1980, Fujitsu began marketing its Japanese word processor which it called the "OASYS," choosing the "nickname" from suggestions solicited from the public. When a comparatively inexpensive general use model, the "My OASYS" was released, sales skyrocketed. The My OASYS was promoted in print and television ads by the very popular Hawaiian-born sumo wrestler, Takamiyama. He was, by the way, the first American ever to win a Grand Sumo Tournament Championship.

We are now putting our technological expertise to work in the development of automatic translation machines which will be able to translate from Japanese to English, and from English to Japanese. A production model has already been shipped. Before long, such machine translation systems will be widely available.

GREAT STRIDES IN THE SEMI-CONDUCTOR FIELD

One of the principle factors behind the success of JEF was a tremendous leap forward in semi-conductor performance. A special characteristic of Fujitsu's semi-conductor development is that the whole effort is directed predominantly toward computers. Since semi-conductors (LSI and VLSI) are the "lifeblood" of computers, this has had a decisive significance. Semi-conductor business at most other companies is based on production for consumer use—household appliances and the like. Semi-conductor quality is not as high as it might be because their objective is to turn out large quantities and supply them cheaply to these primary markets. Fujitsu also did this at first. When a semi-conductor division is an independent entity concerned about their own bottom line, rather than produce a limited number of high performance devices for computers which require painstaking, time consuming design, they will tend to be more interested in selling large quantities of less complicated chips to consumer oriented markets such as television manufacturers.

Fortunately or otherwise, the home appliance division of the Fuji Electric Group was on the weak side and got started late. Despite efforts to sell to this consumer market, they were unable to be price competitive. Since there was no sense in expending energy and resources producing expensive semi-conductors that could not be sold, the decision was made to become a manufacturer specializing in semi-conductors for computers.

This was accomplished by incorporating the Semi-conductor Division into the Computers Division. By putting computer design teams together with semi-conductor design groups, we were able to concentrate our engineers in such areas as integrated LSI memory and logic chips for computer use. As a result, there was an upsurge in the level of our technology.

In addition, the merger in 1968 with Kobe Industry also proved to be beneficial. In the late 1950's Kobe Industry had attempted to move into the consumer electronic industry, and failed. On the recommendation of the Bank of Kobe, Fujitsu came to their assistance. They had a corps of excellent engineers, and we decided a merger at some point would strengthen our own engineering group.

This move was even more effective than we had anticipated and formed the basis for our later development of the M-Series with Amdahl. The distinctive feature of the Amdahl machine was the use of LSI's for all its circuits. Due to the introduction of this technology and the use of a computer to design the circuits themselves, the M-Series turned out to be a highly efficient line of computers.

Today the complexity and precision involved in designing semi-conductors demands it be done on a computer. At the time, our cooperative research with Amdahl for the

M-Series allowed us to make rapid progress in this area. The M-380, which had the world's largest processing capability when it was announced in 1981, represents another order-of-magnitude leap forward.

The course we followed to reach our current state-of-the-art position led from one obstacle to another. During Okada's term as President, semi-conductor yield was poor. Monthly statements continued to show red ink for semi-conductor operations. Finally, due to incredible efforts on the part of our engineering staff, the yield suddenly improved. Just as we reached the point where we could begin to recover our costs, the quantities we were producing could not be sold fast enough, and our inventory began to bulge. Interest cost then became the cause of all the red ink. This was the constant pattern: We solved one difficulty only to be confronted with another.

One day while touring a Hitachi factory with their plant manager, I causally mentioned, "Up until recently we had a mountain of scrap, now all of a sudden we have to bear the interest expense for a mountain of jewels." I heard later that this gave him quite a shock. Yield is the whole game in semi-conductors. If the yield is running around ten to twenty percent and you are able to raise that to over fifty percent before any of your competitors, your costs come way down and you will be able to reap the profits by being first into the market. With the profits earned by increasing the yield faster than other companies, you can then invest in the next round of development and move further ahead. It is what might be called a "benevolent cycle." Semi-conductor and computer manufacturing at Hitachi were separate divisions. Their surprise at our success may—this is just my conjecture—have been due to the fact their semi-conductor people, interested in the bottom line of their own operation, were unwilling to put much effort into producing the complicated and initially unprofitable semi-conductors requested by their computer division people. At Fujitsu, however, because semi-conductors and computers were in the same operating division, we were able to produce high-quality, specialized semi-conductors for computers at a much lower cost. The anxiety this must have caused Hitachi appears to have been serious since it was right about that time Fujitsu and Hitachi joined forces to build the M-Series.

Hitachi's semi-conductor division at the time had already grown too big for them to incorporate it into their computer operation as Fujitsu had done. Instead, they drew the best of their engineers from each and set up a "device development center." Fujitsu's example may have prompted this change.

I should add that later, when Fujitsu's semi-conductor group had expanded its capacity and capabilities, it was made an independent division and given the autonomy to choose its own strategies. The results again were impressive. In short order the transition from 64 kilobit memory chips to 256 kilobit chips was accomplished. A prototype 1 megabit chip was successfully produced, and they have now targetted volume production.

THE CHALLENGE OF VLSI DESIGN
AND PRODUCTION

As a result of the Fujitsu's semi-conductor groups concentration on advanced devices, the value of each chip is approximately twice that of those produced for general consumer use such as home appliance applications.

The most advanced of these devices are those based on gallium arsenide (GaAs). We have already been successful in selling these new gallium arsenide transistors for use in

American space satellites. Progress has also been made in the field of optical transmission devices (high frequency, integrated semi-conductors which convert electrical signals to light). We anticipate rapid advancement in this area which is already profitable.

Another technological development which will be receiving world-wide attention is the HEMT (High Electron Mobility Transistor). The HEMT is a new, high-speed device that operates at an electron-transfer speed fifty times (theoretical value) that of transistors based on silicon used in LSI's and other IC's. Even compared to the gallium arsenide transistor, the fastest of the devices now in practical use, it is ten times as fast. When compared with the Josephson junction device upon which attention has been focused in recent years and which is still under development in our research laboratory, the HEMT operates nearly as fast and has the advantage of being much easier to test.

The Josephson junction device can only operate at temperatures approaching absolute zero (minus 269 degrees) and testing must also be conducted at this low temperature. The HEMT can be tested at room temperature and its performance evaluated. At a low temperature (minus 196 degrees), it approaches the speed of the Josephson device. Thus, HEMT devices are much easier to produce, and research can proceed that much faster. With the Josephson device, which only works at very low temperatures, there are distinct disadvantages, because it is impossible to evaluate the performance until the project is completed. If the development of the Josephson device takes ten years, the HEMT will only require five, and we will have been able to create something with the same level of performance in half the time. This is why we expect the HEMT to be the most appropriate device for the next generation of powerful computers.

The computer industry today is planning the development of super computers (ultra high speed computers for advanced scientific applications). The creation of very high speed devices, an order-of-magnitude faster than those currently available, will be essential for producing these super computers. At Fujitsu the development of new technology such as the HEMT naturally comes from a devotion and commitment to research. But surprisingly, many discoveries are made almost by the way. They are born out of the enthusiasm of the scientists and engineers actively engaged in research. This kind of innovation is not something that can be directed from the top. I think this is a distinctive characteristic of our company.

The development of the HEMT is a good example of this. The principles on which the HEMT is based were brought to light by Bell Laboratories in the States. In this instance, however, they gave no thought to applying this principle toward the creation of a particular device. Many others did embark on a research program to develop an application, and Fujitsu's research team while absorbed in the problem came up with a breakthrough.

JEF was a similar case. I mentioned previously how when I heard Professor Goto's lecture, I said to myself: "Yes, of course, this is it," and urged that efforts be made to create a Japanese language processing feature. In fact, from well before I said anything about it, there was research being done. In the laboratory ideas had been circulating: "Why can't *Kanji* (Japanese characters which originated in China) be used on a computer? Until now we had fallen into the belief that there was something wrong with *Kanji*. That's not the case at all. There is no reason in the world why we can't make a computer that can handle the Japanese language." The ground work had already been laid by independently motivated research. My announcement merely served as a stimulant.

One of the managers responsible for JEF said to me: "It began when a group of young engineers said they would like to tackle the problems of Japanese language processing. They started on it and before we knew it there was the green light signaling full speed ahead. It was a young group and having to think about so many new problems, it naturally whetted their appetites for the development of new approaches and designs." This spirit has spread and been passed down to new members of the company, becoming, I think it fair to say, a Fujitsu tradition.

ENDLESS POSSIBILITIES

People long ago looked up at birds flying in the sky and thought they too would like to fly. In imitation of the birds, they attached wings to their arms and flapped around. Before long the Wright Brothers invented the airplane. Propeller driven planes gave way to jet propelled aircraft, and today we have a space shuttle.

Today's computers are probably comparable to the wings people strapped on and flapped around in. In due course, they will gradually become more and more "human." Add arms and legs to one of these computers and we will have an "intelligent robot." Japan, at present, has more robots in use than any place in the world. They are made to perform a variety of useful operations, but their intelligence is still too low for them to be assigned to more complex, advanced types of work. Before we can have robots do work approaching the level of human capabilities, artificial sight, hearing, and tactile sense must be developed. Then it will be necessary for robots to "recognize" what it is they have seen, heard or touched. Proceeding further, they will then have to make inferences and decisions based on that knowledge.

The level of technology we have today, however, does not come anywhere near the human level with regard to perception, knowledge, etc. Take voice recognition technology for instance. Without programming a machine to recognize a specific voice, only a limited number of simple words—at most ten numbers and "yes" or "no"—can be recognized. If a particular speaker is designated and the specific vocal characteristics of this speaker are recorded beforehand, a computer can recognize only about 2,000 items. This is about the intelligence level of the human child of kindergarten age.

When it comes to reading written characters, if the letters are clearly differentiated, a computer can distinguish and read them. Of the 5,000 to 10,000 characters (*Kanji*) in Japanese, a machine now can read up to about 2,000.

Research on language has moved ahead rapidly in recent years, and simple translations can now be done by machine. In the summer of 1984 Fujitsu began marketing a Japanese-English machine translation system called ATLAS. At Tsukuba Expo '85 there was a demonstration of machine translation from Japanese to English, German and French which attracted considerable attention.

The commercially available system is presently just for English. But for it to be widely used, it will have to be able to handle French, German, Spanish—multiple languages. We are proceeding with the development of machine translation systems for these and other major languages. Imagine being able to travel and communicate freely with people living anywhere on the globe. When these systems are completed, this will become possible.

I frequently travel abroad. On these trips, too often have I seen Japanese tourists who only stare silently at the scenery and buy a bunch of souvenirs. There is absolutely no verbal exchange with the people of the foreign country they have come so far to see. If this situation continues too long, problems are bound to arise. I would love to make it possible for people visiting a foreign country to go out shopping for instance, with a translation device in hand, and be able to chat with the local people about ordinary, everyday matters. Companies are now competing to develop this technology. So I would not be surprised if within ten years a portable translation machine for about $500 becomes available. If I were younger, I would very much like to work on creating such a machine myself.

Recently, with the advances in computers and robots, there has been talk of bio-robots and bio-computers based on the ideas of biotechnology. These are extremely interesting conceptions. Biotechnology, however, unlike our electronics, gets along without the control we have down to the very precise point we call a bit. I do not think we will soon reach the stage where the two—electronics and biotechnology—join and something is actually produced.

When challenging these new frontiers of research, it is very difficult to conduct fruitful research within the narrow scope of companies in the same industrial group. It is clear the joint development must be made with businesses outside the confines of traditional relationships. Although there may be no capital participation or personnel exchanges, increasingly we will hear "That company is the leader in the field. If they are willing, let's work together." This type of joint endeavor with companies beyond traditional alignments, with research the principal tie, will have to be done more and more in the future. Fujitsu, for example, has joined with Toray, Asahi Chemical and Olympus among others, in joint development projects where there have been no special capital arrangements. We expect to be doing this kind of thing to an even greater extent in the future wherever the situation calls for it.

This, I should stress, will not be limited to domestic tie-ups. We are actively considering similar arrangements with foreign companies. As I have already mentioned, in an age where everything from high-end mainframes to home computers are being combined into unified systems, a good system cannot be built if you try to supply everything from within your own group. A much greater degree of freedom in the system is possible if you are not constrained by the limits of a particular industrial group. When joint projects are arranged outside established capital connections, objections may be raised pointing to the possibilities of industrial secrets or proprietary information being lost. This is a problem we have to face, and for which reasonable solutions must be found.

RESEARCH FACILITIES OF THE UTMOST IMPORTANCE

One aspect of Fujitsu's computer business I would like to single out for special mention is the unique set-up we have for research and development. Simply put, this can best be expressed as providing the best possible environment for good research and development. We are often told that Japanese have no originality or that our research is second rate. I would respond this is because all too often a directive, "this particular research has to be done," is given, but the peripheral support fails to materialize. For a researcher, the most important element in a research project—possibly as much as 80% depends on this—is having the right tools for the research at hand. In other words, an environment in which research can proceed smoothly is essential. In a high tech world, without the right environment, demands for inventiveness or originality are unreasonable.

It occurred to me some time ago when I was visiting the Science Museum in Munich, West Germany, that the epoch-making inventions that have left their mark on history down through the ages were the result of an economic environment optimizing the chances for a breakthrough. The right combination of factors allowed light to shine upon the industrial arts of the day. These inventions were not something that just appeared in a flash without any supporting environment. The moral questions aside, the classic example is, of course, military technology. Progress was made because in order to win at war a country drew on its human and financial resources to the fullest extent.

When established businesses are unwilling to back a particular project, it can be set up as an independent "venture business." If it gets the support of venture capital (which closes its mouth but opens its purse) good results often follow. In America, venture businesses are prevalent. I think many of their great achievements might be attributed to this entrepreneurial spirit. To draw a parallel with Fujitsu, one might say we practice what could be called an "intra-company venture business." We value the personal preference conceptions of young employees and provide as much in the way of funding as we can for them to pursue their new ideas.

The HEMT mentioned above is one instance of our success with this approach. The HEMT was developed out of the ingenious combination of two technologies: device engineering and the technology of molecular beam epitaxis (MBE), a crystal growing technique.

In 1975 there was talk at Fujitsu Laboratories of purchasing molecular beam epitaxis equipment. We made some inquiries and discovered that there was not even one of these machines in Japan at the time. The cost was somewhere around a billion yen. The people directly involved were asked what the equipment was to be used for. I learned that it was for producing super lattice hetero junctions on a single crystal in a vacuum by adding very thin layers of gallium, arsenic, aluminum, silicon, etc. in a process controlled by a computer. I thought this would be a direction for future research. The young engineers at the laboratory thought so too: "We are sure this will lead to a breakthrough. We'd like to work up the specifications for the equipment and have Nippon Vacuum Technologies build it. Could you please allocate the funds."

I knew that the previous year at Bell Labs they had attracted worldwide attention by developing a semi-conductor with aluminium, gallium and arsenic using this type of machine. Still I had reservations. There were quite a few questions to be answered. But sympathizing with the tremendous energy of the young engineers, I decided to go ahead and provided the money just as they had asked.

Afterwards, I forgot all about it until five years later, when, in May 1980, our public relations department notified me that they wanted to make an announcement: "Our laboratory has just succeeded in producing a revolutionary breakthrough in semi-conductor device technology. It's called HEMT. We would like to release the news to the papers." Listening to the backgroud I was reminded that I had given the go-ahead on the purchase of a molecular beam epitaxis machine five years earlier. The machine, I was told, had not only been a great help, the purchase had served to greatly increase the morale of the engineers at our research lab. This in turn contributed to the HEMT break-through.

We made a formal announcement to the press on the 19th of June and the next day all the newspapers gave it a big write-up on their front pages. One of the headlines read: "Fujitsu announces development of ultra high-speed transistor. Prospects bright for new computers."

The 20th happened to be the anniversary of Fujitsu's founding. Every year we hold a memorial convocation, and have a company beer party and other events. Thanks to the news, the HEMT was a major topic of conversation and spirits at the party were very high. Young engineers involved in research vowed that they "were not to be out-done," and would surely produce equally fine results. The mood was decidedly upbeat.

I heard that the researcher responsible for the develop-ment of the HEMT was talking one time with an English scientist and the subject of his HEMT discovery came up. He said, "My success with the HEMT development was due to a certain amount of good luck." The Englishman, to encourage him, told him an English proverb which goes, "Fortune favors the brave." I think it is a proverb with impli-cations well worth pondering.

These days I do not really know what our young employees are doing. I'm afraid I do not have the physical energy to be telling them to do this and do that as I use to. When they come to me to ask, "Please give such and such to me to do," with the exception of a few special cases, I tell them all, "Okay, give it a try."

This is the Fujitsu way of doing things which was estab-lished during Kanjiro Okada's term as President. It is from this sense of "we are doing it" that the young find a purpose and worth in their lives. And unless it is done this way, we cannot expect to see creative work.

It goes without saying that it is desirable to maintain a constant research and development effort unaffected by the ups and downs of the business cycle. Even more important is the smooth transition from discoveries made at our research facilities to marketable products in our various departments. It is not a simple step. Too often, for example, an interesting discovery is made in the research lab and brought to the attention of one of the departments in operations with ideas for turning it into a product. The department, then has a tendency not only to reject the suggestions and fruits of the careful research, but to turn around and invest financial and human resources in research more to their own liking. The research division, of course, does not take kindly to this reaction and will respond, "What's the matter? Don't you put any trust in something we have thoroughly researched?" This is the kind of thing that makes managing the research division difficult. (An old, but true story about this very problem concerns radar research during the war. The research laboratory of a company had come up with very promising results but their operations department did not believe them and had them do all the research over. It is a well known story illustrative of this common problem.)

The activity we call research is not something you can dictate to be done in a certain way. There are many routes to the same established objective. Besides, Japanese tend to find accepting something someone else has done exactly as it is, uninteresting. Everyone wants to bring their own originality to bear upon the problem. Actually, unless this natural human attitude is respected, good research cannot be accomplished. In the past, questions in this area caused Fujitsu no small amount of trouble. During Kanjiro Okada's presidency in 1962, Fujitsu Laboratories was organized by merging a union of research and development sections previously managed by separate technical divisions. In 1967, Fujitsu Laboratories Ltd. was established as a subsidiary of Fujitsu Limited. The aim was to strenghten the motivation of the research staff and eliminate the conflicts with the design divisions. It is difficult to evaluate research in process, and we could not afford to have people call something research and just be dawdling around; so we felt that by making it an independent corporation, we could more accurately access and evaluate our research programs.

At Fujitsu Laboratories, research and development is conducted both at the request of our design divisions and on independently established projects. In the former case, the research expense is borne by the division requesting the work, and after completion, the expenditure is figured into the cost of the final product. In terms of personnel, a system has been set up whereby a person is sent from the design division to the laboratory to participate in the research. When the research phase is finished, that person returns to his regular department and sees the project through to the final product release. Because the same individual is responsible for the whole process—from research to final product—there is a continuity of concern and energy which has produced very favorable results.

Research entrusted by the design divisions is largely related to input/output devices. Independently initiated research includes such fields as machine translations systems. The occasional exchange of information between groups involved in different projects as they pursue their goals has also contributed to the laboratories' excellent results. This is characteristic of Fujitsu's way of doing things.

In short, the secret to successful research and development is the careful transition from laboratory results to commercial product: The knowhow must be meticulously transferred; the timing well calculated; and the momentum toward future research not impeded.

Accordingly, although we are often told that the Japanese have no originality, I believe that this is not the case at all. If you provide an environment where research can proceed smoothly and enthusiasm is generated, I am confident good results will emerge. Some will surface as the inspiration of genius and others, just as fine, will be the result of bleary-eyed, persistent, desperate research. Providing the proper research environment, furnishing the necessary equipment, and injecting an appropriate degree of competition are, I believe, the essential components of successful research.

VIII

ACTIVE LEARNING

Rather than ordering young people "Do this" and "Do that" when they ask "Let me do it," the answer should be, "Alright, give it a try."

THE WORK FORCE:
MOVING FROM QUANTITY TO QUALITY

Over the past twenty years in knowledge intensive industries like communications equipment and computers there have been major changes in the composition of the work force. Simply put, the number of white collar workers has increased more rapidly than that of blue collar, and the educational level has risen sharply. In Fujitsu's case, twenty years ago blue collar workers made up 60% of the total work force, the majority being women. Recent data, however, reveals a complete reversal of these proportions. White collar workers now represent 65.8% of the total. During the high growth period, our problem was finding enough people to keep up with the large increases in production output. After the oil shock with the subsequent shift to slower expansion and rising payroll costs, it became more than a question of simply increasing the head count. We began to place more emphasis on hiring personnel who had the requisite intellectual capabilities for work in the increasingly complex world of computers and communications. This is clearly indicated in the statistics.

Since in the final analysis it is individual human beings that make a business work, improvement in the quality of the employees raises the efficiency of corporate administration and production and is directly related to the overall progress of the business. A company's human resources are its greatest asset. With this in mind, I have done everything in my power to cultivate and maintain our excellent human resources.

A personal experience in the United States led me to this way of thinking. Over twenty years ago I had the opportunity to tour IBM's facilities in Poughkeepsie and Endicott. I was very impressed to see how much effort IBM put into educating its employees. They had a special research department working on various educational and training methods. The training techniques being developed were not only for the education of IBM's own employees. They were also studying ways to teach customers who used their computers. At the time, the truth dawned on me: "We have only been concerned with manufacturing products but this education thing is clearly very important. If we don't set up facilities like this for education we're sure to fall behind."

In a separate wing of the same factory I was visiting, they had a "training center." It was filled with audiovisual equipment and people working on developing efficient educational resources and curricula. There was no doubt about the seriousness and enthusiasm they brought to their tasks. It was then I decided "Up to now we have thrown all our energy into the production of machines; in the future we have to develop people before we build machines. If we are able to develop people, good machines will naturally follow."

As you know, the quality of blue collar labor in America is hardly ideal and the ethnic variety of the work force poses great problems. With this labor force, what does one have to do to produce a uniform product? What kind of tools are required? How do you provide maintenance for products in the field? IBM was conducting research to answer these kinds of questions.

When employees received IBM training, they actually left their work place and devoted full time to the training in a defined format. With one eye on your job and only one devoted to study, it is not possible to achieve very much. Real training cannot be accomplished that way.

This IBM tour became the impetus for Fujitsu's step by step creation of a special department responsible for education and the beginning of regular employee education training programs. We observed a rather interesting phenomenon when these training programs were first introduced. They were conducted by the computer operations division and we found employees were not following the training plan very well. We then put the personnel department at company headquarters in charge of employee education and "click" everyone all of a sudden was trying their very best. We asked ourselves the reason for this sudden change. Evidently, it was because the personnel department was in charge of employee evaluations, and low scores in the training program could have repercussions when it came to salary reviews. We really did not expect there to be such a big difference in employee response. Human psychology is a strange thing: It seems, I'm afraid, results are not to be achieved unless there is some kind of real incentive.

For education to be effective, those receiving the training must recognize its intrinsic merit or it degenerates into a kind of play. Since we had experts in our computers division, they were assigned as instructors. When they had to instruct their own colleagues, however, we found they received a lackadaisical response. Order was hard to maintain: It got so bad members of the class would sit on the desks, smoking during the presentations. This all changed, things tightened up considerably, when the instructors were sent from the personnel department.

"HEY! GIVE IT A TRY"

Education is something which should originate in an individual's desire to study. It cannot be forced on someone from without. Unless it grows out of a person's motivation for self-improvement not much can be expected. The source of education can be found in each individual employee's will and effort to develop their own knowledge and abilities. The premise is they will strive for personal growth by applying new skills and talents to their work. This is the reason for any educational endeavor. The role of on-the-job training (OJT) and various intensive educational programs is to encourage and assist the individuals in their efforts to improve themselves.

Therefore, in cultivating human resources it is not enough to simply train employees according to some set educational curriculum. Study in the work place is also very important. Passive education—listening to lectures and reading—is not really effective. The fundamentals may be learned in this way, but once a certain level has been reached, further on-the-job training is essential. It is this passive-active combination that produces results.

In my own case, ever since I joined the company I have felt like "the company president." Which is to say, as one of the first employees in the company, none of my senior colleagues (with the exception of the factory managers) did the design work I was involved in or had a very good feel for customer's needs. In this sense I was the "first senior colleague." In those early days at Fujitsu, because of our relationship as a supplier of switching equipment to the Communications Ministry (the predecessor of today's Nippon Telegraph and Telephone Corporation) the upper management ranks were filled with ex-officials from the ministry. They were people who had, as we say in Japan, "descended from heaven:" They left government service and took a position in private industry. In the technical arena, many of the engineers came from our parent company, Fuji Electric, where they had turned out motors and power distribution panels. Temperaments differed and everything did not always go so smoothly. Nevertheless, as younger people joined the company in increasing numbers I found myself as one of the "old hands" being thrust to the forefront. Some of the people who had come from government and Fuji Electric resigned or retired and there I was "feeling like the company president."

At that time, of course, we did not have the well developed educational programs in place that we do today. There was no time for formal training and I always found myself studying whatever was at hand, learning from the immediate work that had to be done. Even today, try as I might, that is a habit which is hard to break. Whatever the project, I would learn by immersing myself in it, trying something out, failing sometimes, succeeding sometimes, always accumulating experience. Anybody can read a book and understand the theory behind something. University professors are the classic example. When they lecture, a theory is presented logically and clearly—it is very easy to understand. A problem arises when you try to actually make something following the theory: It does not always go according to the book.

I was not at all convinced that a machine built according to the theories I had learned at school would perform well. When, in fact, I had the opportunity to put those theories to a real test, there was a significant gap between the theory and actuality. Most papers and articles that are published deal only with the successful aspects of some particular research; the failures do not find their way into print. The current state of knowledge in a field is limited by this practice of "putting the best face forward." The blunders and failures which should also be recorded hardly ever see the light of day. Watching professional golfers on television, you might tend to think that all you have to do is hit the ball and right to the pin it goes. Everybody's experience, however, tells them it is not quite that easy to do. Only with extensive practice—which entails failure after failure—does it become possible to hit the ball with precision of a pro. In the same way, unless you actually give it a try you cannot understand how to make a good product. Without rolling up your sleeves and doing it you will never develop the skill.

In a previous chapter I described my involvement with the "Capital Defense System." At the time I felt very keenly how important it was to deal with whole systems. It was a good object lesson. At what altitude will the enemy aircraft approach? What has to be done in order to shoot it down? I felt the necessity for a total system which could incorporate all the critical variables. Because it was a military project and there were no budgetary constraints, I was fortunate enough to be able to conduct a great variety of experiments.

In the course of these experiments problems would arise. I experienced directly how coming to grips with these problems became a motivating force driving up the level of my engineering capabilities. This is why I often tell young employees, "Hey, give it a try. Then let's hear your objections. Not having really done anything yet but read a few books and talked to a few people, don't pretend to know how it's going to turn out. If the results are just as you'll say they will be, I'll stand on my hands and walk around the room."

The literature on a particular topic can be used for "reference" but it should never be trusted entirely. Many years ago, I was conducting an experiment on something that was a published and publically acknowledged "fact." A senior colleague inquired why I was doing "such a useless experiment." The truth of the matter is that unless I give something a try and think "Yes, of course, that's it!" I am just not satisfied.

THE MOTIVATED FUJITSU EMPLOYEES

People in our industry often say, half in praise, and half with distaste, "Fujitsu employees work like they are crazy." Quite frankly, I suspect that they are right. It is not, however, forced on them from above. I'm afraid it is a natural consequence of conscientiously responding to our customer's requirements. In the computer business, late delivery is unacceptable. Once a customer places an order, the computer is figured into their plans and becomes involved in their whole range of business operations. Before delivery there has to be a thorough warming up period, and the machine must be fully tested to insure there are no problems. This preparatory period takes more time than you might imagine. Considerable effort is required before the final "okay" is reached. Unless employees really hustle, they will not reach this okay point before the delivery deadline.

In this regard, nothing could please me more than to hear "Fujitsu employees work so hard." It is for this reason we have earned our customer's approval and are able to produce highly reliable computers.

If it were IBM, and their machine was not functioning properly, the customer's resigned response would likely be, "Well, since it's the great IBM, it must be a really difficult problem to solve." If, on the other hand, Fujitsu were to deliver a computer that was not working well, because we are pursuing rather than leading in many areas, the response might well be a blunt "No more orders from us." This is why we at Fujitsu have to put extraordinary effort into our work. Ultimately the impetus behind this drive is a desire "not to be defeated by IBM."

Unless people are placed in extreme conditions, not much in the way of wisdom will be developed. Sitting at a comfortable desk in a nice environment tends to dull the edges and douse the sparks in people's minds. Whereas, I believe that standing at the edge of a precipice and trying to find a way to live there at the brink focuses the mind and brings forth the beginnings of wisdom. Thus, even when you think "it just cannot be done" you have to give it a try anyway. It is this final exertion, or holding fast that develops the strength to get you one stride ahead of the next person. If you are content with just doing what the next person is doing, you will never surpass your elders. This is why then Fujitsu people are always placed in difficult positions and have to spend day after day close to the edge. To outsiders it may look like "giving people rough treatment," but if we did not do so, the knowledge and wisdom we seek in individuals would not be developed. Had we not done so, IBM would still be number one in Japan.

This philosophy has become a Fujitsu tradition. I think

it has its roots in the independent development of our technology. Had it been technology learned or purchased from outside, this feeling would not have emerged. Designing and building our own technology was arduous but the strain drew forth the energy to persist and push on. It might not be the best example, but consider someone who loves to play mahjong. He can stay up all night playing and not get tired. In the same way, if employees feel "this is our work, this is something we are developing," even if they put in long hours, they will not feel it is a tremendous burden. It is work they want to be doing. Should they, however, be directed from above "Do this" and then "Do that," the response is likely to be, "Why do we have to work so late."

In short, if there is a feeling of responsibility, a sense of the importance of responding to customer's needs, and the determination not to be defeated by IBM, even if it means some degree of overexertion, things will get done. It is hard for anyone who has not actually been in this situation to understand.

The group that joined the company around the time I did was the last to have to struggle laboriously with technology from outside. The careers of people who came after coincided with Fujitsu's period of internal technological development. The joy these people felt at being able to open up new areas for research and development—just the fact that they could do their own work—must have been more than consolation for the strain and overwork they endured.

I remember meeting one of my old friends some months after his son became a new Fujitsu employee. The first thing he said was, "Just what kind of education are you doing at Fujitsu?" Asked why he was concerned, he responded, "That youngster has only been with Fujitsu about six months and he's talking like he had the responsibility for the whole company on his shoulders. He returns home from work late in the evening. I thought he might have been out playing mahjong but he wasn't. He was working. How did you do it? How could he have changed so quickly?" I told him, "We're not doing any special training. It's just that we're building computers with our own knowhow and doing everything we can to please our customers. Your son's attitude is not unusual. It's natural that this happens." Too often we hear, "What has become of young people these days?" Fujitsu's youngsters, however, appear to be faithfully carrying on the traditions we are so proud of. Nothing could delight me more.

When giving young people work to do, we know it is essential they also be given responsibility and the freedom to develop independence and self-motivation. It is also extremely important that the responsibility placed on them be within the scope of their capabilities. Dropping responsibility on a person that they cannot handle can destroy that person. Care must be taken to achieve the right balance. I, myself, was not gifted with any especially extraordinary talents. I was an average, ordinary businessman. I sense pretty much about the mean among Fujitsu men. Therefore, my own experience tells me intuitively that Fujitsu has been doing things right.

A UNIQUE MID-CAREER EDUCATIONAL PROGRAM

I have been describing Fujitsu's general approach to employee education and training. Here, I would like to introduce one of the unique features of our educational system: The program for our forty-five-year-old employees. This program was instituted in 1979 with the following principal objectives:

A. The fostering of comprehensive managerial and administrative skills in areas beyond the specialized fields of each individual expertise in order to develop executive personnel able to take on the responsibilities of our domestic and international operations and management duties in our affiliated companies.

B. By offering an opportunity for supervisory personnel to acquire advanced managerial techniques, develop the ability to respond effectively to the ongoing diversification and growth of our company.

C. Insure the optimal utilization of human resources by conducting a multidimensional evaluation of each individual's qualities and abilities. A thorough evaluation will serve to elucidate the best future course for the individual and allow us to plan the optimal allocation of our human resources.

D. Provide an opportunity for self-reflection and edification in order to nurture a work force imbued with a broad, humanistic perspective.

The three month program, involving one to two hundred employees at a time, consists of two main components. The first two months are devoted to general studies and training. The third month has a more specialized curriculum. (Facilities for the program are located in the Numazu Factory and the Kamata Systems Laboratory.)

A system of life-time employment is prevalent in Japan and most companies have a mandatory retirement policy for employees between the ages of fifty-five and sixty. Since the average life span for Japanese has increased to around seventy, the problem of finding new employment after this first retirement has become a major social issue. One of the objectives of our mid-career education program is to prepare employees for this eventuality long before they are faced with the problem directly.

During this three month program provisions are made for each participant to have a consultation with one of the company directors. I will never forget my first chat with an employee in this program. As he sat down I could see his hair was beginning to thin on top. He said to me, "You know, I've worked at Fujitsu now for more than twenty years and until this moment I haven't had a chance to talk directly with the president. I'd given up the thought. Today, being able to sit and talk with you like this makes me very happy."

These informal conversations last only three to five minutes and are usually a brief exchange of questions and answers. When this employee spoke these words, I really felt them go straight to my heart. He had just wanted an opportunity to talk with the president, and I thought to myself about moments I had wasted in leisure—there were so many people I should meet. Even so, despite what I felt, there are physical limits to what one can do—I was unable to suppress my chagrin.

The people who take part in this program can be divided into three main groups. The first is the department manager class. These are people whose careers are advancing much as they would wish. The second group includes the section manager class. The third is made up of those individuals who did not qualify on the exam to receive section manager training.

The majority of this last group are people who have worked hard for the company, but, perhaps because they put too much emphasis on individual tasks, did not develop enough knowledge in the area of administrative or managerial skills. Many of them are wonderful human beings who, because they have excelled at their jobs, have significant things to contribute with their observations. I have been amazed, in fact, by their acumen on more than one occasion. Nevertheless, we offer this training program so that they can open up for themselves a path that will bring them satisfaction and fulfillment during their remaining years with Fujitsu; a path that allows them to develop and contribute rather than become a burden to the company. Once they give this program a try, most feel it is a valuable experience.

Basically, I think middle-age employees should be treated in the following manner. Do not plan on helping an employee who reaches a mid-career crisis and then comes asking for assistance. Instead, before—not after—the crisis is upon them, initiate discussions to see what can be done to alleviate or avoid such a crisis. We considered the age of forty-five to be the turning point. At forty-five there is still the desire and energy to make a new start and get on with the next phase of life.

After a person turns fifty, their desire begins to fade and a sense of dependency grows stronger. The requests for help finding post-retirement jobs become more urgent. And then should Fujitsu recommend them for a job, we tend to hear nothing but complaints: The pay is too low, or the work too hard. At that point there is not much we can do. At forty-five there is still time; by fifty it is too late.

I have often assisted employees in finding jobs after retirement from Fujitsu. There is no more unpleasant, less rewarding task. Even though you know the individual you are recommending will not be of much use, you still urge that he be hired. The party being pushed cannot object directly, but you know in private they are expressing their displeasure. The personnel people know this and do not want to be involved. I would at least like to be able to say,

"Here is a person with these particular strengths" and see him off in good conscience.

There are some, of course, who impudently say, "If you had only done this for me in my thirties." I just remark that people in their thirties can make these decisions and changes themselves. After forty-five, the situation changes. Because it is someone's last chance, we have to lend a hand.

Pure necessity is another factor that should be mentioned in connection with our educational programs. In the United States there are recruiting firms which can gather for you any number of people with the requisite abilities. No such independent management recruitment services are available in Japan. With our lifetime employment system, all the necessary personnel must be either selected from the pool of current talent, or trained and developed from the time they enter the company as youngsters. Over the course of the next decade, Fujitsu will have to continue to build additional factories, each employing more than 1,000 people. We are also actively expanding our network of offices both in Japan and abroad. Furthermore, every year we establish approximately ten software companies. It is clear that we will need people to manage all these facilities. We intend to make the best possible use of our veteran middle-aged employees.

The actual content of our program is based on case study methods, with lectures and seminars conducted by professors from such institutions as Keio University's Business School. The hard schedule, similar to that of an American university's business school, leaves no time for a leisurely beer or T.V. in the evenings—everyone is too busy with assignments and preparations. Over the course of the program, self-confidence is built and people emerge feeling they really want to "give it a go."

A fine example of this attitude was an employee who, when he finished the program, was asked to manage our manufacturing facility in San Diego. He enthusiastically took up the challenge, and when I met him in California he told me, "That training course really put us through the ringer. It was tough, but it gave me a lot of confidence and I have been able to put what I learned to good use managing the plant here."

We spend over one billion yen (about four million dollars) annually on this mid-career training program. In the near future it is expected to increase to about two billion yen which will represent a significant outlay for the company. Virtually everyone wants to see the program continue and since I think it produces results far outweighing the expense, we intend to continue this unique educational system.

BATTLING WITH ILLNESS

Five or six years after joining Fujitsu, I became extremely busy with a research project on radio controlled weapons conducted in conjunction with the Army and Navy. As the Second World War intensified, government control of the economy was put into effect, and it was no longer possible to grab a bite for lunch at a restaurant in town. I can remember running around in a hurry looking for a place to have lunch but finding all the restaurants either closed or without food to serve. It got to be two o'clock and all I could do was return to the company to continue my work on an empty stomach. A series of days like this back to back finally took their toll on my health.

One day at work I became very anemic and left early to visit my regular doctor. Amyloid infiltration of the lungs was his diagnosis. Amyloid infiltration was the first stage of tuberculosis. In those days, we did not have antibiotics such as streptomycin and the mortality rate for consumption was very high. The doctor's diagnosis was quite a shock—the equivalent of being told today that you have cancer. The doctor, a family physician, was a pediatrics specialist, so he suggested I be examined by a doctor specializing in tuberculosis and introduced me to a well-known clinic. The doctor there told me, "There is no effective medication for this disease. All you can do is eat good food, rest and recuperate. It's useless to visit a doctor for periodic checkups. What you have to do is take a year off from work and convalesce at home."

In the meantime, Fujitsu's President Wada became concerned and arranged for me to be examined by the company's medical insurance physician. This doctor did a cursory examination and pronounced me fit for work: "You're not sick. What's the meaning of this when everybody else is working. You can go to work tomorrow and everything will be fine."

Three doctors with three different diagnoses: I did not know which one to believe. The third doctor, in particular, having been recommended by President Wada, could not very well be ignored. And, too, the prospect of taking a year off did not at all agree with my disposition. Finally, I decided on a middle course: I would recuperate for three months. During those three months, I spent idling around at home, I put on a great deal of weight, so much in fact it was shameful. My complexion and general health improved, but I could not afford to take anymore time off and was soon back at work. In no time at all, the furious pace had me trim again.

The rest, however, had not completely cured me. After

the war, I was faced with necessity for major surgery. As you can well imagine, the food supply situation immediately after the war was not good, nutrition was poor and this definitely affected my physical condition. Nevertheless, I managed to cover up and put off doing anything about it so as not to have to miss work. It was not long, however, before my wife developed pleurisy after giving birth to one of our children, and we found ourselves making trips to the hospital together.

My wife's symptons were rather severe. She was not able to swallow any food. It was almost as though she had one foot in her grave. I used to have to pass a funeral parlor on my way to work. Everytime I passed I wondered when I would be requesting their services. They were very depressing days.

It was then that a friend came up with an unusual suggestion. "There must be some reason why both you and your wife have been hit with tuberculosis. I have an acquaintance that does divination. Even if you think there's nothing in it and you are just being fooled, please go and have an onomancy performed." Onomancy is a type of divination based on the number of strokes in the characters of a person's name. I do not put much faith in this type of thing but at that point I was grasping at straws and agreed to my friend's suggestion. I had my name examined by Dr. Shunkei Nakajima of Kamakura. Dr. Nakajima's verdict was that it was absolutely necessary for me to change my name. He wrote the new name for me, Hidemasa, in characters on a sheet of paper.

The name my parents had given me, Teizo, is extremely difficult to read and write correctly. Anybody could read and write the name Hidemasa. I was sure it was just a hoax, but I sent everyone announcements with my new name.

The strange thing is that, much later, in 1957, when I was manager of our sales office in Osaka, I paid a call on Dr. Nakajima and he advised me to once again change my name. Now, names are not something you run around changing constantly and I said as much. Upon being told that even a pen name would suffice, "Taiyu" became my third and present name.

By chance, about a month after I changed my name the first time, relatives who had gone to America sent us a package of thirty bottles of streptomycin. The medicine was not available anywhere in Japan at that time. Thanks to this medicine, my wife's sickness improved dramatically and since then she has not had any serious medical problems.

During one of my visits, while my wife was in the hospital, I asked to be examined to see what had happened to my previous tuberculosis. An x-ray was taken and about a ten millimeter vomica, or abnormal cavity, was discovered in my lung. "If you do nothing about it, within five years you'll be on your back. The probability of your living another ten years is zero. It would be best to have the surgery done right away," was the doctor's pronouncement.

Since I was in no hurry to die, I resolved to do as the doctor advised. It was major surgery involving the cutting of four ribs. Thanks to the sure scalpel of Dr. Masao Tsuzuki, the eminent Tokyo University physician, since then I have had no problems with my lungs.

My next affliction—sometimes I think the god of sickness hovers over me—involved my stomach. My stomach has gone under the knife three times. The first was in 1959 for a duodenal ulcer. Given the option by my doctor of going to the country for three months to rest or having surgery performed (in which case it would take one month to recover) my impatience led me to choose the one month alternative. That was a mistake that had repercussions.

At that time, for ulcers or whatever, if the stomach was bad they removed about two-thirds of it. For ten years or so after the operation, my condition was pretty good, but then I started to have some bleeding. They inserted a camera into my gastric tract but were unable to find the source of the bleeding. I discovered later that when the original surgery was performed there was bleeding from a narrow part connecting the duodenum and the small intestine. I underwent examinations at various hospitals but no one was able to locate the cause of the bleeding. I was hospitalized for two to three months, recovered naturally, and went back to work. This whole process was repeated a number of times until one day my stomach ruptured and I had massive hemmoraging.

Told that if nothing were done it would be curtains, I had emergency surgery performed. Had a more careful check been done before the operation, it would have been farewell to my stomach problems, but because it was a half-finished job, I later had to have a third operation.

When the surgery was performed, they did not suppress the secretions of stomach acids sufficiently so that the part where the incisions were made eventually weakened and ruptured again. The condition was aggravated by the fact that the ulceration was in a narrow, obscure portion of the stomach. With the third operation, they were able to successfully suppress excess secretions of gastric acid. I recall the doctor poking fun at me: "Your stomach has been under the knife three times now—it's a real custom job." Fortunately, in the years since that last operation I have been fine.

That I have been able to continue working and not become a human vegetable is due, I guess, to a strong constitution and, who knows, perhaps changing my name has had something to do with it. I used "Taiyu" at first as just a pen-name but have since changed even the official registry. When I first went to Family Court to have my name changed in the official records, the applicaion was rejected. I was informed, "We do not accept name changes for the purposes of onomancy." I explained that the characters of "Teizo," the name given to me by my parents, were difficult for people to read and discovered even the judge could not write it correctly. After a variety of ploys, in 1962 I finally succeeded in having my name changed officially to Taiyu.

LEARNING TO DELEGATE RESPONSIBILITY

Looking back over my period of struggle with illness and the serious thoughts it provoked about human life, I believe it was all to the good. Despite the fact that I injured my health working spartan-like, demanding days, I had absolutely no feelings of resentment toward the company. I was more concerned while I was away recuperating that my work would be taken away from me. I also began to see it would be better to delegate more of the work to others rather than trying to do everything myself.

In the mid-career training program at Fujitsu, employees leave their work place for a period of three months. The participants' attitudes change as they go through the course. During the first month away from their jobs, they generally feel, "If I'm not present, there will definitely be problems." The second month they realize, "Hmm, the company seems to be doing just fine without me." By the third month they become very concerned: "If I don't watch out I'll lose my place entirely." They cannot wait to finish the program and get on with their jobs—with a renewed vigor and enthusiasm. This was not something we planned from the outset but seems to be a natural consequence of their instincts as businessmen. I had the same feeling during my bouts with illness.

In the old days before travel by jet was possible, when someone went abroad for study, it took a long time because they went by boat. In the pre-war period, Fuji Electric established technology transfer agreements with the German company, Siemens. For my senior colleagues, a six-month stay in Germany was their ticket to advancement. Men chosen to go were looked upon with envy. There was, however, one person who refused the offer. Asked why, he responded, "If I spend half a year over there, my work here will be passed on to somebody else." I wondered at the time if that was his real reason, but had to smile at the irony when I felt the same way during my periods of convalescence.

I eventually realized that, when it came right down to it, the work I was doing at Fujitsu was just a small fraction of the total picture. I find myself these days telling our middle management people: "This might be a little hard to take, but as section managers it's something you should know. You might think that you are well-respected by your subordinates. The fact of the matter is half, if not most, of the more capable people under you would be refreshed and invigorated with you gone."

When I had finally recovered from my illness and was back on the job, there was a mountain of work that had to be done. Since I was still not back to full strength, I could only get so far and then my body would refuse to go any further. It made me realize it was impossible to accomplish everything I wanted to do by myself. I recognized the necessity for marshalling appropriate groups to achieve specific goals in the various projects we had undertaken.

During the period of my convalescence, I had some free time on my hands. I took the opportunity to visit a famous *shiatsu* masseur and, at the urging of a friend, I attended some lectures on self-cultivation given by a leader of one of the new religions in Japan. I heard all kinds of stories and found the experience very interesting.

The teacher of this new religious sect was known for being able to cure people with his preaching. Their center, located on a hilltop, has a low roof with sunlight permeating the large rooms. The mood was the exact opposite of what one usually finds in the main hall of a Japanese Buddhist temple with its high rooflines and dimly-lit interiors. When I arrived at the center for a meeting, the assembly room was already filled with a large number of followers.

Presently, the teacher, a man who looked like the first Zen patriarch, Bodhidharma (Daruma), appeared. His voice resonant with confidence, he began his sermon. An inspired, keenly intuitive speaker, he had tremendous persuasive power. Listening to his sermon and chanting the mantra, "Praise to the Sutra of the Wondrous Law of the Lotus," before long the audience seemed to be hypnotized. They moved around as if in a trance. I noticed one of them moving rather strangely and inquired what his affliction was. The person I asked responded by pointing to his thigh. I was impressed by the spectacle of this strange therapy, but it did not seem to have any effect on me. The cold I had at the time was unaffected and I felt nothing like the hypnotic state others appeared to be experiencing. When I asked the teacher about this, he said, "You look at me from morning to night with eyes of doubt. People who think only, 'Why? Why?' will not be affected. Please try to be a bit more innocent." When I did not say anything he continued, "You are trying to swim upstream, fighting the current. If you don't let yourself go with the flow, hardships are many and benefits few."

He really got me with this one. It really was excellent advice. After that I was able to abandon the urge to try to do everything myself. I henceforth made a greater effort to delegate responsibilities to people who had the will and energy to get the job done. It was definitely a better way and I shifted my thinking accordingly.

Naturally, this delegation of responsibility to younger employees was not something that could be accomplished overnight. It was a gradual process. Seen from the outside it might have even appeared that I had lost my drive. The truth is, as a result of this process the company has become more stratified and the structure does not require me, at my age, to be dashing around all the time.

IX

TECHNOLOGICAL
WONDERS

*As we move into a new age of computers for the general public,
outmoded institutions and laws will change. We should, however,
never lose sight of the fact that human beings, not computers, will
play the leading role in the new information age.*

THE POPULARIZATION OF COMPUTERS

Science and technology have made remarkable progress
in various fields in recent years. From the point of view
of someone involved in the information industry, I would
like to express my thoughts on what the future may have in
store.

Japanese society and the national economy are now experiencing an "Information Revolution" that promises to
alter the shape of the future in significant ways. We are on
the verge of an age which will see the mass utilization of
computers. The major question Fujitsu faces today is how
to meet the challenges this rapid computerization of society
will bring. Having been involved in the production of a wide
range of computers and communications equipment, Fujitsu is in the fortunate position of being able to provide
every level of machine from super-computers and main-

frames to mini- and micro-computers. To draw an analogy with Mt. Fuji, the scope of our operations extends from the snow-covered peak to the broad plains at its base and the mountain is expanding rapidly upward and outward. On one hand we are proceeding with the development of powerful high speed super computers and the visionary "Fifth Generation" machines which correspond to the snow-clad summit. On the other, we have begun to enlarge and diversify the base with office, personal, and home computer systems. Judging from what we have seen in the progress of semiconductor technology, in the near future, processing power will increase rapidly and the cost will continue to drop, so that anyone who wants to will have prodigious computing power at their fingertips. If we can come up with clever, useful software, demand has the potential of expanding indefinitely.

In this field today, IBM is playing the role of leader. A few years ago, in 1980, IBM entered the personal microcomputer market, beginning a major internal transformation as they lay their foundation for strategy in the 1990's. Multinational giant that they are, IBM had always taken a rather reposed, gentlemanly posture. Recently, from our standpoint at any rate, IBM seems to have become totally indifferent to appearances. In the past, IBM activities were based on a clear, forthright philosophy which guided their direction. Because of this, it was relatively easy to read the direction and obtain some idea of their objectives. IBM has now undergone an abrupt change. They are moving into the broad base of mass market computers and peripherals. Having dealt before only with machines they produced themselves, they have begun to buy some hardware and even software from other companies and are, at times, acting like a trading company.

Our response has been to introduce new broad-based products, to open up new sales channels and continue our search for new, more effective marketing techniques. For example, although Fujitsu hitherto had no connection to the retail business in home electronics or office equipment, we created a new sales distribution network to sell word processors, office computers and facsimile machines as well as provide our customers with software support. It may take five years to get the system running smoothly in high gear, but we are in this for the long haul. Since we are now entering a period in which we expect to see a dramatic increase in office automation (OA), with effort, I have every reason to suppose our new sales organization will be successful.

The advancement of computers will have a great effect on our personal lives and businesses. There are some people who question whether this will really contribute to the future happiness of humanity. I, for one, do not think there is any reason for pessimism.

We live in an automobile age. We go everywhere by car: Shopping centers, supermarkets and even barber shops. Even in Japan, I know of people who have stopped going to a particular barber because it did not have a parking lot! The automobile has become so much a part of modern society, life without cars is unimaginable. Not so long ago in Japan, a driver's license was considered a "special skill" on employment applications. Now, you are made to feel foolish if you do not have a license.

These days, if you know how to use a personal computer, you are given points for having a "special skill" when applying for a job. Just as happened with the driver's license, however, in less than ten years, if you have never used a personal computer, and apply for a job, I am sure your chance of being hired will be nil.

The cost of personal computers is much less than that of a car, so the pace of popularization should be that much faster. Young people today are gradually becoming less and less fond of concentrated thinking and working out mathematical calculations. The computer is just the tool for them. Because it is not terribly expensive and unobtrusive, the day is coming when homes will have not one, but a number of computers here and there around the house for family use. If the automobile replaced the horse, the computer will replace the "thinking cap."

In 1983, the highly respected consulting firm, IDC, Inc., which specializes in forecasting trends in the United States, predicted that by 1986 dollar volume production figures for home and personal microcomputers would surpass those of general purpose mainframes. The personal computer market is clearly undergoing explosive growth.

While in some respects there is the danger people may become lazier, the use of computers permits the efficient and rational use of time and resources both in one's personal life and in business. The time and energy saved can then be used for more creative endeavors. Up until now, people had to adapt themselves to computers. I believe we are about to begin the process of designing computers to more closely respond to the needs of human beings.

Contemporary science and technology is expanding its horizons continually but a single individual can only master a small part of a given field. Yet, as problems become more complex, a broad understanding of the interrelated issues is of paramount importance. Therefore, we look for a scientist with both a deep and broad grasp of his field. Such individuals are unfortunately very rare. One solution to this problem is the use of a computer as a stand-in for the expert we seek—a computer that can respond to our queries based on a wide range of information at its disposal. This is what we call an "expert system."

In the United States an expert system in the medical field called MYCIN has been developed. When a doctor examines a patient he first asks about the present symptoms, takes a medical history and so on. If necessary, he may gather additional data by taking the patient's temperature or blood pressure reading. Based on this data, he looks for a similar disease or problem he has encountered in his previous medical practice. If the data is insufficient, he continues his examination. He might take an x-ray, do an electro-cardiogram, or have a blood sample analyzed. If he finds a close parallel with a past case history, he can give a correct diagnosis.

In recent years, however, with the specialization in medical science and increasing differentiation of specific diseases, a doctor cannot have been exposed to the symptoms of all the identifiable diseases nor is he able to remember so many different case histories. If we feed a computer with all this information on case histories and symptoms and then enter the data on the symptoms of a patient, the computer can respond with a possible diagnosis based on this extensive data base. Since in most instances a particular set of symptoms does not agree exactly with the model case history, the computer can prompt for more information and suggest additional tests be conducted.

In other words, the patient's examination would be conducted while the doctor consulted the computer. For the doctor, it would be as if he had a specialist to confer with, greatly reducing the possibility of a wrong diagnosis.

The strengths of this expert system, MYCIN, really come to the fore when we reach the stage of prescribing therapies. So many new drugs have been discovered recently it is not easy for doctors to accurately recall which medication is indicated for a particular illness or what the side effects may be. A computer that tells them which drug should be used is a tremendous aid to their medical practice.

The function of the computer does not end there. As new case histories of disease are encountered, if a similar example does not already exist in the data base, this new data will be added or existing data revised to include the new case. In human terms we would call this "learning." With expert systems, this process gradually increases the intelligence of the machine. Eventually it is able to assist in the diagnosis of even rare, complicated diseases. Nevertheless, we must not forget it is always the human physician, not the computer, who makes the final diagnosis. Regardless of how advanced and "intelligent" the computer, the master is ultimately a human being. First-rate doctors will eventually be those who are able to skillfully utilize computers.

Expert systems built around computers are not limited to the field of medicine. They will gradually play a role in many areas of human activity. They may be applied to Office Automation (OA), for example. Today's OA systems such as facsimile, word processors and electronic mail do not require a very high level of machine intelligence. In the office environment, computers are used primarily for ordinary financial and administrative data processing. This will change as the intelligence level of computers rises to a new plateau and personal desk top machines become more widely used. When electronic files can be called up inexpensively, we will see business management expert systems similar to the MYCIN system in medicine. Top management and executives will be able to confer with these systems for assistance in business planning and managerial decision making. This, I believe, is the essence of the office automation revolution now in process.

HIGH EXPECTATIONS FOR INS

Nippon Telegraph and Telephone, looking ahead to the 21st century, has begun work on the centerpiece of its vision—a nationwide, high-speed digital communications system known as INS (Information Network System). Fujitsu, as a major communications equipment manufacturer will be able to assist in the development of this INS. Naturally, we have high expectations for this new venture in telecommunications.

The typical home in the society envisioned by the INS designers will have a variety of computers and telecommunication equipment. First, of course, is the telephone. The home of the future will have a number of multi-function phones with such features as automatic dialing, answering and call forwarding. (Call forwarding is a service which allows an incoming call to be automatically forwarded to another designated phone when there is no one home to receive the call.)

Next, there will be a facsimile terminal which can send and receive written or printed text, diagrams and so on. The facsimile is especially appropriate for Japan because it permits the easy transmission of *Kanji*, the thousands of characters used to write Japanese. Facsimile has additional advantages: Information can be sent even when the recipient is not there to receive it; it is fast and a hard copy record of the transmission is produced.

The third will be a home data system. It will consist of a keyboard for entering data into a computer and a printer which can output various kinds of information in standard Japanese (including in *Kanji*). The home terminal will not be as complicated as a typical business device. It will have to be simple enough for even children to operate.

Finally, there will be a home video display device to obtain information when a hard copy is not required. Regardless of whether televisions currently in use are adapted for this purpose or a separate CRT device is used, families will be able to call up on screen a great variety of useful information.

In addition to these basic devices, other kinds of equipment with a wide range of features will find their way into the home of the future. These homes will be wired so that devices can be plugged in the same way we use electrical outlets today. Lines will be connected to a communications processing center similar to our present local telephone switching stations. Instead of today's copper wire lines, transmissions will be over high-speed digital optical fiber cable. In the INS environment, people will be able to access large databases from their homes, have text or graphic information sent to them, and produce hard copies when necessary with their printers or facsimile machines. The hardware for all this has already been developed.

Although the initial step towards implementing the INS plan was taken in the fall of 1984 with the introduction of an experimental system in one district of Tokyo, the overall vision is a vaguely defined outline with goals projected into the 21st century. We would like to see more concrete, detailed plans as soon as possible so that we can develop our own business plans accordingly.

For example, the INS plan calls for the "investment of thirty trillion yen over the next twenty years." In our industry, "twenty years" from now is the unfathomable future—the dream world. Practical business plans are established on a three or five year basis; at most ten years. We have to have detailed information on the interim stages; a precise project schedule is necessary.

Another factor the INS plan must not fail to take into consideration is economic feasibility. The President of NTT, Dr. Shinto has also often raised this issue. Regardless of how attractive and convenient the hardware available, if the cost of using the system is too high, it will be difficult to obtain popular acceptance. INS services will remain beyond the reach of the general public.

During the 1982 "Fujitsu Office Automation Show," we introduced our Tele-video Conferencing System to the public. The system connected our Kamata Systems Laboratory and Numazu Factory. Both locations have a large number of software experts and frequent meetings between the two groups were required. Constant travel was both time consuming and costly. Therefore, we set up a Tele-video Conferencing System which enabled visual and voice communication as well as simultaneous transmission of hand written documents from multiple-points. Meetings could be conducted just as if all the participants were in the same conference room.

It took considerable effort to get NTT to agree to setting up this system on an experimental basis. Kamata and Numazu are about 120 kilometers apart, whereas NTT's regulations permit video transmission only up to 60 kilometers. Another problem was the telephone rate structure in Japan. The difference between local and long distance rates is much greater than in most other countries. Consequently, the cost for long distance tele-video conferencing becomes prohibitively high. Even so, because we considered this tele-video conferencing an integral part of our plans for technology development, we are using it fairly often. The high cost, however, has put a bit of a damper on promoting the system for general business use.

In the States, where space satellites are used and optical fiber cable installation is proceeding fairly rapidly, long distance tele-video conferencing for businesses has been in operation since the spring of 1982.

IBM, Aetna Life Insurance Company, and Comsat General joined to form the Satellite Business Systems Company (SBS). Subscribers of SBS service have only to install a parabolic antenna on the roof of their building and two-way video-transmission allows them to hold long-distance conferences which feel as if a face-to-face meeting were actually being conducted. Because satellites are used, the charges are not dependent on distance, and I am told relatively inexpensive service can be provided.

I would like to mention that Japanese manufacturers (Fujitsu and NEC) have sold a substantial amount of equipment to SBS. Fujitsu, for example, has supplied a "Burst modem"—a satellite communications variable modem; while NEC has supplied ground stations. In other words, Japanese technology is seeing its full potential being put to use in the United States. Conditions certainly exist for doing the same in Japan. Unfortunately, compared to the U.S., Japan is behind in its planning and it is not at all clear when tele-conferencing will become generally available.

The 1985 Tsukuba Science and Technology Exhibition in Japan has presented some interesting responses to the question (and theme of the exhibit), "As we move into the information age, how will technology affect our daily lives and the environment we inhabit?" I expect it will prove to be a pivotal moment in the course of technology in Japan.

X

COMMUNICATIONS REVOLUTION

Since the liberalization of NTT, the role Fujitsu is expected to play in the communications field has been changing from a mere maker of equipment to a total system supplier of integrated networks including VAN, LAN and satellite communications.

THE INCREASING IMPORTANCE OF BUSINESS COMMUNICATIONS

Japan's present telephone network, which is the basis of our national communications system, was put into place after the war under the auspices of Nippon Telegraph and Telephone Public Corporation (NTT). Government objectives for postwar communication development have by and large been realized; Japan's nationwide telephone system is on a par with systems in other advanced countries. The exceedingly rapid pace of technological advancement in the area of communications, however, has raised important questions concerning the present systems' capacity to respond to new demands. The need for advanced multifaceted communications and information services in business and industry has increased dramatically. With its current organizational structure, operating policies and regulations, our communication system will not be able to respond effectively to these new demands.

For this reason, existing communications policies are undergoing a thorough reevaluation and revamping. New measures planned include the lifting of restrictions on the use of the public communications network, the early realization of a high-speed, high-capacity, fiber optical cable network, and the utilization of satellite communications systems. Furthermore, we are moving forward to open up domestic telecommunications, hitherto under the monopolistic control of NTT, to competition among private companies.

In October 1982 the second step toward liberalizing the use of lines for data transmission was taken. Although some restrictions and conditions are still in effect, the measure was a decisive step in the right direction. Provisional, temporary measures were also enacted to permit third-party vendors to offer value added network (VAN) services to small and medium size businesses.

Advanced countries of the world are now moving into a period Dr. Alvin Toffler characterized as "The Third Wave." In order to realize the full potential of this wave of innovation in telecommunications, the present organizational structure and laws impeding progress have to be changed. The concept of a local area network (LAN), for instance, has become increasingly popular. In addition to personal and desktop computers, word processors and facsimile machines, today's offices use a variety of advanced office automation equipment. All this is in the process of being tied together into one system with fiber optical cable or other local wiring. Unfortunately, once you try to get beyond the confines of a particular local area network and develop the system further, present regulations make this rather difficult to do.

Twenty years ago as we entered a period of mass use of automobiles, expressways were built to accommodate the increased traffic flow. If, in a similar way, we do not make timely provision for a public electronic communications network we will face a variety of pressing problems. Business communication is a case in point. Over the past couple of years, office automation has progressed rapidly but the advances have all been internal. Should a business try to interconnect with outside, they find the communication circuits insufficient and the inherent limitations of the system frustrating their efforts. Internally, they may be able to transmit text and graphic information simultaneously over optical fiber cable, but the network outside is unable to handle this level of advanced communications.

When we look at the prospects for the future we see that despite NTT's ambitious plans for the large scale Information Network System (INS) mentioned above, the system is not scheduled to be in operation until 1990 and full service (including video transmission) is not planned until 1995. With this time frame, the system envisioned will not be able to catch up with the world's rapidly expanding telecommunications needs.

I have on many occasions emphasized the necessity for quicker, more decisive action and have recently been pleased to see concrete steps being taken to both open up the domestic telecommunications system to private enterprise, and liberalize restrictions on the use of the existing network.

A new telecommunications industry bill has been passed in the Diet to relieve the heavy restrictions imposed by the previous telecommunications allied business law. The bill provides for the following changes:

1. The establishment of "Type I and Type II Telecommunications Enterprises." Type I Enterprises can have their own communications lines and equipment. Type II Enterprises can lease lines and equipment from Type I operators and offer value-added communications services.
2. Type II Enterprises are further divided into: (a) Special Type II, which are expected to provide large-scale nation-wide VAN service and (b) General Type II, which are expected to provide communications services mainly for designated industrial groups.

Type I Enterprises are subject to the approval of the Ministry of Post and Telecommunications. Several Type I companies have already been established. Type II Enterprises involve simpler registration systems. As for foreign capital participation, the Type I group will be restricted to up to one third foreign ownership of stock; Type II Enterprises are, in principle, free of any restrictions.

When these changes go into effect, Japan will be among the countries of the world with substantially liberalized telecommunications regulations. Although the demand for telephones has leveled off, in its place demand for data communications and other digital transmission service has been growing steadily. Legal obstacles have supressed this growth but when the above liberalization measures are put into effect, I think we can reasonably anticipate explosive expansion in the Japanese communications industry.

We now have a customer base of tens of thousands of companies. Of these, more than one thousand are large corporations. The largest companies will probably move toward setting up their own independent communications systems. In view of these developments, Fujitsu has already launched a number of efforts in the area of information communications service and new media technologies. The development of a large scale Value Added Network (VAN) is one example. We have already built a communications system for internal company use. With the data and experience gained from this in-house network, we are prepared to provide our customers with a variety of services now possible due to the opening up of the domestic communications market completely in April 1985.

Fujitsu celebrated the fiftieth anniversary of its founding in June 1985. Just before that, in the fall of 1984, our new headquarters building was completed. On this occasion, in place of the analog network we had been using, the new building has 6.3 Mb/s high speed digital lines which are connected to a comprehensive companywide integrated digital network.

This new multi-media information network which makes extensive use of new Fujitsu products and advanced technologies has voice (telephone), data, image (facsimile), and picture transmission capabilities. It will integrate our in-house office automation and become, in effect, an internal "Corporate INS."

The knowhow gained from the experience of developing this integrated network at Fujitsu enables us to create products and provide systems which fully serve the needs of our customers. As the demand for integrated networks increases in the business community, Fujitsu is well positioned to provide a "Corporate INS" utilizing the most advanced information processing and networking technology.

Based on our integrated digital network, Fujitsu has also moved into the field of VAN services. The new information-communications services supplement existing communications for businesses with value added telephone, facsimile and TV-teleconferencing services. Our large scale Value Added Network has come into use since late 1985.

One of our subsidiaries, Fujitsu F.I.P., is now providing small scale VAN services. When the plans I have outlined are realized, they will, of course, be linked with the larger network, as will the members of the FACOM Center Association, the computer association with the largest number of participants in Japan. Member computation centers will be linked to the network and undertake the development of applications so that specialized, fine tuned services may be made available.

SATELLITE COMMUNICATIONS IN JAPAN

Along with the opening up of the domestic telecommunications network to competition among private companies, as a leader in Japan's electronic communication industry we are also very interested in developments in satellite communications systems. As we move into an information economy, the communications network infrastructure is going to play an increasingly important role. The distributed processing, office and factory automation, currently being introduced throughout the business world and the networks to link these new technologies organically will require high speed, high volume communication circuits as soon as they can be realized. Satellite communications can satisfy these requirements.

In June 1982 Yoshihiro Inayama, Chairman of Keidanren (The Federation of Economic Organizations), the most powerful round table in Japan, asked me to chair "The Committee on Information and Telecommunications Policy"—one of the Federation's standing committees. Concerned as I was that if nothing were done to speed up the development of Japan's communications network we would not be ready to meet the challenges of the information society already upon us, I readily accepted the offer.

Twice a year, in the spring and fall, Fujitsu hosts a social gathering for representatives from the approximately three thousand companies which are our principal customers. Some of the attendees are also members of the Committee of which I am chairman. At the Fujitsu gathering there were repeated requests to move ahead quickly with communication satellite launches and to do so at prevailing international costs. I was in complete agreement. Consequently, in January 1983 a subcommittee, the "Special Committee on Communication Satellites" issued an advisory report entitled "On the Early Realization of Private Sector Use of Satellite Communication in Japan."

The subcommitte report pointed out the main bottleneck to actualizing plans for satellite use is the problem of how to launch satellites. In February 1983, Japan's first practical communications satellite, the CS-2a was sent up with a domestically produced rocket, the N-II. It was a small model (350 kilograms) and its capacity rather limited. In a crisis or peak period it would not be able to handle simultaneous use by a large number of users. With present Japanese rocket technology, however, it is not possible to launch heavier payloads such as large communication satellites. The report stressed that it would, of course, be desirable to launch satellites with our own technology, but if this was not feasible in the short term, an alternative was to turn temporarily to a foreign country for help. As a temporary measure this would not necessarily run counter to the basic spirit of "independent technology development."

The recommendations of the subcommitte became the focal point of a dispute in the upper echelons of the Keidanren: One side favoring independent technological development, the other opting for temporary help from abroad. The independent development faction emphasized the fact that "independent development had been determined to be our fundamental national policy." They argued, "We cannot claim to be a first class nation if we do not have the capacity to launch our own satellites." Due to their insistence, Keidanren published another advisory report in March. This time the recommendation took the following form: Although the situation abroad should be given due consideration, in view of the national importance of securing a satellite communications network, we strongly urge that the Japanese government actively take on itself the expense of independently developing satellites and the necessary launch vehicles.

Despite the suggestions put forward in this report, the current situation still requires communications development be geared to the government's budget rather than the budget being prepared in accordance with progress in research and development. The deficit financing we have had in recent years further aggravates the problem; funding in fiscal 1984 was kept at previous levels. If the present trend continues and measures are not taken to permit the use of satellites, we are likely to see a quality gap begin to appear between Japanese and American industries dependent on information technologies. There was definitely a sense of crisis in the air.

Soon after the Keidanren report, there was progress in discussions concerning the problems of NTT's equipment specifications and opening up their bidding to foreign supplies. A proposal was put forward suggesting the purchase of an American satellite. On this, the independent development faction and the help from abroad faction reached a compromise. The plan called for the government to use its resources to proceed along the lines of independent development in accordance with the general policy for satellite development outlined in March 1978. The private sector, however, would be free to use its own funds to purchase satellites and the government would then make every effort to provide the "environment and arrangements" to allow the full utilization of these private sector satellite communications systems. The "environment and arrangements" in this context meant the necessary legal provisions. Use of a communication satellite by a private corporation will require the cooperation of various government agencies and the revision of national communications laws.

When the telecommunication laws are revised to facilitate the move from monopolistic control of domestic telecommunications by NTT to competition among private companies, private sector businesses will benefit greatly from the liberalization of the regulations. The opening up of communication circuits on the ground, the spread of optical fiber transmission systems, and launching and use of communications satellites, will undoubtedly have a profound impact on the communications revolution in Japan.

NTT's Information Network System (INS) plan is extremely ambitious but it is very long range—full scale operations are not scheduled until the twenty first century. The next satellite, the CS-3, is to be launched in 1988; and the following one CS-4, not scheduled until 1990.

At Fujitsu we are much more concerned with what can be realized in manageable time frames. We are particularly interested in plans for a group of private companies to launch advanced communications satellites in the near future.

The revolutionary changes in the telecommunications

industry will set the stage and provide an excellent opportunity for Fujitsu to expand its activities in this area. We are in a position to do so because of our experience in digital technology developed over the years in computers. Until recently, communications equipment was primarily analog; the move to digital communication devices will enable us to take full advantage of the high quality digital technology refined for use in our computers. It appears the time has come for Fujitsu to take its turn at center stage.